THE THRIVING INTROVERT

EMBRACE THE GIFT OF INTROVERSION AND LIVE THE LIFE YOU WERE MEANT TO LIVE

THIBAUT MEURISSE

CONTENTS

Do you despise small talk? Do you frequently refuse to answer your phone? Do you wish you could skip the parties you're invited to? If any of these sounds familiar, you might be an introvert. Don't worry, you're not odd or defective. In fact, you're full of wonderful qualities that are much needed in today's society! You simply need some time on your own to recharge your battery. I invite you to view your introversion as a gift, and the best way to offer it to the world is by embracing who you really are deep down.

This book will be a great fit for you if any of the following is true:

- You want to learn more about introversion and its implications on your life.
- You're sick of being told to talk more, become more outgoing, or attend more social events, and you want to embrace your introversion wholeheartedly.
- You want to create a life that supports your introversion.
- You struggle with social events and want to become better at interacting with people while staying true to your introverted self.
- You want to be able to leave parties without feeling guilty, awkward, or pressured to stay.
- You want to feel comfortable in your own skin and thrive as an introvert.

If you can relate to any of these statements, this book is for you!

Why This Book

This book is the book I wish someone had given me when I was younger. To be honest, I didn't know what introversion was until a few years ago. And I only learned about it when I started delving deeply into personal development.

Under different circumstances, I would probably have spent my entire life ignorant of introversion and its implications on my life. Sadly, that's what happens to many of us. Even when we believe we understand introversion, our idea of it is often vague. As a result, we have difficulties designing a life that truly matches our introverted personality. If anything, we blame ourselves for our introverted behaviors, and may even feel ashamed of ourselves.

While you can find many great books on introversion out there, they generally fail to offer you practical steps to help you redesign your life. After reading them, you may feel inspired or empowered in some ways, but without a practical action plan, they will leave you unsure of what to do next.

Even worse, these books often encourage you to act like an extrovert, perpetuating the idea that something is wrong with you. My guess is that you don't want to be told you should behave like an extrovert, am I right?

My goal with this book is to explain what introversion is, and to provide you with practical exercises that will help live the life you were meant to live as an introvert. Although in some occasions I will challenge you to move beyond your comfort zone, I don't want you to behave like an extrovert. Instead, I want you to use the gift of your introversion to make your biggest contributions to the world while being as happy as you can.

More specifically, my aim with this book is to:

- Help you deepen your understanding of introversion
- Encourage you to fully accept your introversion and remove any feelings of guilt or shame

- Offer you an opportunity to reflect on your own introversion
- Entice you to take concrete actions towards redesigning your life, and
- Inspire you to live with your introversion to the fullest and make your best contribution to the world.

I understand that your time is precious and I have done my best to make this book as straightforward and practical as possible. To encourage you to take action, I've created a free workbook that you can download for free at the following link:

http://whatispersonaldevelopment.org/introvert

I hope you will make good use of it as you redesign your life. You can also use the workbook available at the end of this book.

If you have any difficulties downloading the workbook, contact me at thibaut.meurisse@gmail.com.

INTRODUCTION

To be honest with you, I longed to be an extrovert for many years. As a youngster, I wished I could go to parties and have tons of energy to talk, interact, and enjoy meeting new people. At times, I even wished I could be the life of the party. I imagined how many more friends I would have and how much more popular I would've been if only I could have been more extroverted. No doubt about it, I envied extroverts, and to a certain extent, might still envy them today.

There were countless times where I did my best to be as interesting as possible only to be ignored within five minutes because I didn't have the energy to maintain small talk. I would then become invisible to the extent that it seemed pointless to have opened my mouth in the first place. Have you ever experienced anything like that?

I've found myself in conversations where I have nothing to say more often than I'd like to admit. It happens most when I'm talking to members of the opposite sex. It's a little strange. I read a lot and have a pretty good sense of humor, but I can turn into a really boring person at parties.

Often, I would return from parties feeling depressed. I kept thinking I needed to be smarter, more attractive, more interesting, and more charismatic. It felt as though I was never good enough.

At one point, I even Googled "how to become more interesting!"

Maybe you can relate to that? I used to chastise myself for being too shy to socialize, and often blamed it on fatigue. I grew to resent extroverts for their ability to maintain conversations in loud and busy environments. Although I knew trying to become the life of the party was near to impossible, I couldn't admit it to myself. This self-defense mechanism may have been a way for me to avoid addressing my problems and embracing my true personality.

At first, I thought my issue was lack of confidence, assertiveness, or leadership skills. Although this was true to a certain extent, it wasn't the whole story. At the time, I didn't fully understand what it meant to be an introvert. In a world where extroversion seemed to be the norm, I was trying hard to put an end to my introversion. It turned out to be an impossible task, but it took me quite a while to realize that fact.

∼

Action step

On a scale of 1 to 10, how true are the following statements? Rate yourself using the workbook.

1. I hate small talk, but I enjoy deep conversations.
2. I get tired if I stay at a party for too long.
3. I feel like everything I say should be meaningful and often refrain from talking for this reason.
4. I prefer one-on-one, or small group conversations over talking in large groups.
5. I need to spend time alone to recharge my battery.
6. I think before I speak.

7. I have difficulty thinking when in a group. I think best when I'm on my own.
8. I usually listen more than I talk.
9. I dislike interruptions.
10. I hate conflict.

1

UNDERSTANDING INTROVERSION

> *What constitutes an introvert is quite simple. We are a vastly diverse group of people who prefer to look at life from the inside out. We gain energy and power through inner reflection, and get more excited by ideas than by external activities. When we converse, we listen well and expect others to do the same. We think first and talk later. Writing appeals to us because we can express ourselves without intrusion, and we often prefer communicating this way. Even our brains look different than those of extroverts.*
>
> — LAURIE HELGOE, AUTHOR OF INTROVERT POWER.

Many extroverts don't understand what it means to be an introvert. It's not easy for introverts to understand extroverts, either. However, the real problem comes when introverts don't understand themselves and wind up thinking something is wrong with them. Although inaccurate, this conclusion actually makes a lot of sense, especially when you look at some of the existing definition regarding introversion. I was shocked by how negative some of them were. Read on for some of the most unsettling ones (but don't feel too depressed, we're going to bust those myths in this book).

- The Dictionary of Psychology states that introversion is, "... orientation inward toward the self. The introvert is preoccupied with his own thoughts, avoids social contact, and tends to turn away from reality."
- Webster's New Collegiate Dictionary describes introversion as, "... the state or tendency toward being wholly or predominantly concerned with and interested in one's own mental life."
- In what is perhaps the most negative definition of all, Webster's New World Thesaurus claims that the words 'brooder', 'self-observer', 'egoist', 'narcissist', 'solitary', 'lone wolf', and 'loner' are synonyms for 'introvert'.

Judging by those definitions, being an introvert doesn't sound like much fun! In fact, it sounds like a pretty bad thing to be. This begs the following questions:

- Why are introverts so different from extroverts?
- Is it possible for introverts to become extroverts, and
- Is there any reason that they should?

∼

Action step

Before we define what introversion is, take a moment to write your personal definition in the workbook.

(*Section I. Understanding Introversion - 1. Your personal definition of introversion.*)

∼

Introverts vs. Extroverts – The Genetic Factor

Whether we're introverted or extroverted seems to be largely determined by our biology, which means that we can't change it—it's a part of who we are. That said, introverts are capable of acting like extroverts and vice versa, but only for a limited time. This, of course, requires a person to return to their natural state to recharge their batteries.

What distinguishes introverts from extroverts is the way they create and consume emotional energy. Extroverts need a lot of stimulation from the outside world. Without it, they start losing energy and begin to feel bored, lonely, or tired. Introverts need less external stimulation and time spent in social situations will tend to deplete their energy. This in turn forces them to withdraw and spend time alone to rejuvenate themselves.

It's crucial for introverts to understand that being introverted is NOT the same as being shy. Although there is some correlation between the two, they are two different things. Not all introverts are shy. Conversely, some extroverts are shy, which can be especially frustrating. If you're a shy extrovert, you want to talk but you can't! We'll touch upon shyness at more length later in this book.

The "Why" Behind Responses to Stimulus

There are actually scientific physiological reasons why extroverts need more stimulation: they're more sensitive to the neurotransmitter dopamine than introverts. In fact, the dominant neurotransmitters of both groups are different: introverts use acetylcholine as their primary neurotransmitter, while extroverts rely on dopamine. Acetylcholine is created through feeling and thinking, and its presence increases focus, enhances memory, and fosters a sense of well-being. It could be said that introverts auto-stimulate by spending time thinking, observing, or contemplating.

Extroverts, on the other hand, need to create more dopamine, which often requires adrenaline. Increasing activity and seeking out stimulation are both efficient ways to ramp up adrenaline. The need for dopamine and adrenaline is a major reason why extroverts tend to take bigger risks than introverts. Risk-taking provides that extra stimulation that extroverts need. They are more reward-oriented and tend to get bored when left alone for too long. As a result, they tend to lose focus and feel worse than introverts when under-stimulated.

In, *The Introvert Advantage*, Martin Olsen Laney, Psy.D. wrote the following on how the use of different neurotransmitters can explain differences between introverts and extroverts:

> *I think the link between which neurotransmitters travel what pathways and how they connect with different parts of the autonomic nervous center is the master key to unlocking the temperament puzzle. Whereas extroverts are linked with the dopamine adrenaline, energy-spending sympathetic nervous system, introverts are connected with the acetylcholine, energy conserving parasympathetic nervous system.*

Further experiments indicate that introverts are more easily stimulated than extroverts. This sensitivity explains why, when put in a noisy or crowded environment, introverts end up being overstimulated, while extroverts thrive.

In a 1967 experiment, Eysenck placed lemon juice on the tongues of people who he identified as introverts and extroverts. He wanted to identify any intra-group differences in rates of salivation. As he expected, during this test, introverts produced more saliva than extroverts, showing a tendency for introverts to be more aroused by sensory stimuli.

In another well-known experiment, introverts and extroverts were asked to participate in a challenging word game. The game involved learning through trial and error. Participants were required to wear headphones that emitted noise and were given permission to adjust volume as they saw fit. On average, extroverts adjusted the volume to 72 decibels, while introverts choose a lower volume of 55 decibels.

Interestingly, the study revealed that, under these conditions, both extrovert and introverts were equally stimulated and played equivalently well.

More surprisingly, when extroverts played the game at the noise level selected by introverts, and vice-versa, both extroverts and introverts underperformed. Each group need significantly more attempts before completing the game. In short, extroverts were under-stimulated, and introverts over-stimulated, which ultimately led to subpar performances.

The bottom line is that introverts, are more easily stimulated than extroverts. We'll perform at our best under moderate sensory stimuli. On the other hand, extroverts will need to be exposed to more stimulation to be able to thrive.

It is important to note that, although most people think introversion and extroversion are the only two options, they actually exist on opposite sides of a continuum. This means it's possible to be an ambivert, or rather, someone who has aspects of both introversion and extroversion. So where would you put yourself on the continuum?

The story of Professor Little

The following story of professor Little is a good illustration of what introversion is and why we must learn to manage our energy effectively.

Brian Little was a former Harvard University psychology lecturer and recipient of the 3M Teaching Fellowship, one of the most prestigious awards a teacher can receive. His students loved him and his lectures often ended with standing ovations. He would frequently sing or make jokes during the classes. He sounds like an extrovert, doesn't he? Well, he wasn't! That couldn't be further from the truth. He was deeply introverted and would spend his free time reading and writing or scoring music in his house, which was located in the Canadian woods.

One day, Professor Little visited the Royal Military College Saint-Jean on the Richelieu River to give a speech to a group of military officers. His speech was so well-received that they invited him each year.

There was one major problem, though. Once his speech ended, they invited him to join them for lunch. It was a nightmare for Professor Little. He had another lecture to deliver in the afternoon and needed some "me" time to recharge his battery. Fortunately, he came up with a great idea. He invented a passion for ship design and asked if he could go for a walk along the river to admire boats instead. You can imagine his relief when this enabled him to successfully decline the lunch offer.

He continued to do this each year and take walks along the river to recharge after his speeches. One day, however, his speech was moved to a different location. He panicked. How would he find a quiet place to rest? He used the last card in his hand, which was the restroom. He barricaded himself in a bathroom stall to avoid interactions with others.

Does this sound familiar to you?

Professor Little's story illustrates that, as introverts, we can act as extroverts for a while, but will eventually need to recharge our batteries. So, if you need to deliver a speech, do a Facebook Live, or go to networking events, you can do it. Just make sure you schedule time to recharge your battery.

The Key Characteristics of Introverts

Now, let's have a look at several primary characteristics shared by the vast majority of introverts, who tend to:

- Spend time alone to replenish themselves
- Dislike small talk but enjoy deep conversation
- Prefer small groups
- Think before they speak
- Require an invitation before they speak

- Avoid speaking until they feel they have something important to say
- Listen more than they talk
- Talk a lot when the topic is something they're passionate about
- Choose depth over breadth (they would rather know a few people very well than know several people casually)
- Keep their enthusiasm and excitement for themselves and share only with people they know very well
- Prefer to know a lot about a small cluster of topics than know a little bit about a wide range of topics
- Need alone time to think (rather than having to endure brainstorming sessions)
- Dislike interruptions
- Be uncomfortable with conflict, and
- Need a lot of preparation before addressing an audience and have difficulties speaking for long periods of time.

Debunking the Myths: What Introverts Are Not

There are many myths surrounding introversion. In this section, I'd like to spend some time debunking the most common ones.

Myth 1: Introverts need to be fixed

Fact: Introversion is not a mental disorder. In 2010, there was a proposal to include introversion in the *Diagnostic and Statistical Manual of Mental Disorders,* which is considered the Bible of mental health diagnoses. As with anything, introversion can coexist with mental health issues, but the proposal was rejected. Unless you're so introverted that it keeps you from functioning on a daily basis, you have nothing to worry about.

Myth 2: Introverts lack social skills

Fact: Social skills can be learned, and, unless markedly shy, introverts can communicate with others just as well as extroverts. They tend to be good listeners, which often gives them an edge over extroverts.

Myth 3: Introverts don't care about other people

Fact: Introverts are as interested in people as anyone else, and are often more interested in people than most. This is part of why they tend to shy away from small talk. Introverts would much rather get to know people on a deeper level. As Laurie Helgoe, author of *Introvert Power* explained, "Let's clear one thing up: Introverts do not hate small talk because we dislike people. We hate small talk because we hate the barrier it creates between people." Well-said!

Myth 4: Introverts don't like to talk

Fact: This may seem true in big groups, but when it comes to small gatherings and one-on-one conversations, introverts can (and will!) talk a lot. This is especially true if they know a lot about the topic at hand or feel strongly about it.

I may not talk much in group settings, but if I'm with one or two friends it might be hard to shut me up! I've definitely had to remind myself to talk less at certain points, and there have been a few times where I've had a friend inform me that I'm talking a lot. It's always a surprise to me and my first thought is, "Seriously? I had no idea!"

However, as is the case with most introverts, this all depends upon how well I know the people I'm talking to. Once the group starts to exceed five or six people, I begin to talk considerably less. One-on-one conversations are my favorite form of communication because they allow me to learn more about a person. What are they passionate about? What are their values? What are their concerns? What are their dreams? And so on and so forth. While I can't speak for every introvert on the planet, I can say that the majority I've met get a kick out of conversations like that.

Introverts internalize, extroverts externalize

 Extroverts often incorrectly assume that introverts are suffering. Introverts internalize problems; we like to take things inside and work on them there. Extroverts prefer to externalize and deal with problems interactively.

— LAURIE HELGOE, AUTHOR OF INTROVERT POWER.

Introverts like to internalize things. We like to think problems through in their mind rather than discuss them with other people. We prefer to look within to solve our own problems rather than share our problems with other people to find a solution. We are at our best when we can think alone in silence. We don't do nearly as well when we're expected to brainstorm with a group and come up with great ideas on the spot.

Similarly, we like to think before we talk, and have generally a lot of difficulties speaking without notice. On the other hand, extroverts speak first and then, refine their thinking as they talk. It is not to say that one way is better than the other, but just that introverts and extroverts express themselves differently.

While in some cases overthinking can be an issue for introverts, we generally are fine the way we are and don't need to be fixed.

Introversion doesn't equal shyness

Many people have difficulties differentiating introversion from shyness. However, these states are not the same, and it is important that, as introverts, we differentiate the two.

Being an introvert, it refers to the way we create and consume emotional energy. It doesn't mean that we lack self-confidence or are afraid to talk to people. If that's the case, it's a separate issue, because people of all personality types can, at times, struggle with confidence and fear.

Many introverts will actually talk a lot during deep conversations, but find small talk draining. The feeling is we should talk only when we have something valuable to say, not just because it's required of us. Forcing themselves to speak when they don't want to requires a major effort on their part and will quickly deplete their energy. Other forms of stimulus that extroverts often enjoy, such as noisy places, bright lights, crowds, or unfamiliar situations will also drain their energy.

As an introvert myself, it took me a while to differentiate between my introversion and shyness. As I gained more confidence over the past few years I discovered that I'm not a particularly shy person. I don't necessarily feel shy in large groups of people or when engaging in chit chat, but I still avoid talking when I don't have the energy for it. Certain situations require more energy than I have and it is that, rather than shyness, which keeps me from being the chatterbox I have sometimes wished I was. Over time, I've become progressively more aware of the vast differences between introversion and shyness.

When I go to a party, I usually don't know who I should talk to. There's not enough time to get to know many people and I'm not fond of casual conversations. I usually end up having a one-on-one conversation with a few different people (this is the best option for me, provided I'm talking to interesting people!) or wandering awkwardly from group to group, exhausted and unsure of what to do. That, of course, is the worst-case scenario. Introverts don't get energized through socializing in and of itself, but we can get pumped up and even intense when conversations turn to topics we're passionate about.

I can't stress enough how important it is to understand the difference between introversion and shyness. When people learn this difference, it gives them an opportunity to reassess whether they're actually shy and enables them to break free of guilt. Working on self-confidence is hard enough on its own, so don't make it even more difficult by confusing introversion and shyness. Doing so can lead to wasted time and energy trying to change something that can't be changed, which will ultimately end in discouragement.

It's not abnormal to feel tired after spending lots of time with people. You're not tired because you're shy, need to get out more, or need to get used to talking to people. You're just introverted, and there's nothing wrong with that.

It's okay if you can't talk at a meeting without preparing beforehand. It's okay if people around you seem like geniuses because they can deliver eloquent speeches at the drop of a hat. They may not be any smarter than you. There's nothing to worry about if you can't think clearly while in a large group. I've noticed that it's very hard for me to come up with really good ideas or think deeply when I'm part of a group. I do my best thinking in solitude. You don't need to feel bad if you have a hard time with chitchat or if you don't feel like talking. And if people find you boring or dull because you don't talk much, that's okay, too.

I feel that introverts tend to seem shy because interacting with people is taxing for them. As a result, they have less experience talking to people than extroverts do, and thus have a steeper learning curve than extroverts when it comes to building social skills. On top of that, extroversion is the norm in many countries, even though introverts account for fifty percent of the world's population. Unfortunately, schools and offices aren't designed for introverts. Many introverts spend their lives being told that they should talk and socialize more, which often leads to guilt and feelings of low self-esteem that extroverts are less likely to experience.

That said, be careful not to hide behind your introversion. Be sure to break loose from your comfort zone from time to time.

I understand that differentiating introversion from shyness can be tricky. Here's something I want you to try for the next two weeks: whenever you interact with people, take time to notice how you feel. For instance:

- Do you feel shy and awkward, or are you simply not in a talking mood?
- Are you feeling drained or timid?
- Do you feel more comfortable with one-on-one conversations, or do you feel awkward, timid, and shy regardless of how many people are involved in the discussion?

Try to identify the feelings that come up during each of your conversations. If you continually examine your feelings and behaviors, it'll be much easier to tell the difference between shyness and introversion.

~

Action step

Using your workbook, complete the following exercise (*Section I. Understanding introversion*):

~

- Write down your relationship with introversion (ex: I feel ashamed, I feel guilty, I feel frustrated etc.).
- Differentiate introversion from shyness by asking yourself: Why aren't I talking? Then write whether your reasons are based on shyness (feeling scared and uncomfortable) or introversion (feeling too low on energy). For shyness write "S", for introversion write "I".
- Write down your expectations regarding this book. Why did you buy this book and what do you want to get out of it? (e.g., improving my relationship with my partner, becoming better at networking, acceptation my introversion etc.)

2

OWNING YOUR INTROVERSION

Unfortunately for introverts, we live in a world that is primarily designed for extroverts. Extroversion is the dominant model of normalcy and many introverts find it difficult to fit in. Many of us try hard to become extroverts, only to end up frustrated and exhausted. We're told we should talk more, be more social, and take more initiative. Sometimes, we are even seen as snobby, aloof, or boring!

However, introversion shouldn't be seen as a burden. It's not something that has to be fixed, nor is it anything to be ashamed of. Quite the contrary, introversion should actually be embraced. As introverts, we have a lot to contribute to the world. As noted in the previous chapter, it's estimated that roughly fifty percent of the people in this world are introverted to varying degree. Who would have guessed? Extroversion is given so much attention and praise you'd think extroverts account for the majority of the population. But that's simply not true.

Introverts aren't powerless creatures who need to buck up and act like extroverts to meet societal standards. If, after millions of years of evolution, introverts still account for fifty percent of the population, it is clear we have our role to play in society. That's pretty important, and we can't be ignored! Millions of years of evolution can't be wrong.

In this section, I'll encourage you to embrace your introversion and throw off any guilt, shame, or frustration you feel regarding it. As an introvert, you have a role to play, and that role doesn't involve pretending to be an extrovert. That would be pointless!

~

Action step

Before we get started, use the workbook to answer the following questions (*Section II. Owning your introversion - 1. Your biggest challenge*):

- What is my biggest challenge as an introvert?
- What could I do to overcome it?
- What is the one thing that would have the biggest positive impact on my life?

~

Why your assumptions on introversion matter more than you think

> Begin challenging your own assumptions. Your assumptions are your windows on the world. Scrub them off every once in while, or the light won't come in.

— ALAN ALDA, ACTOR, SCREENWRITER AND AUTHOR.

We all have assumptions about life. We expect things to be a certain way, and we have specific beliefs on how we think we should behave. As an introvert, you hold many assumptions that you may be unaware of. These assumptions can prevent you from embracing your introversion. A telltale sign of an assumption is the use of the phrase "I should". When you use that phrase, you're likely stating an assumption. So why not take a few minutes to think of all the assumptions related to your introversion?

The expectations you have regarding your behavior can create unnecessary suffering in your life. When you believe you should behave like an extrovert, you'll feel bad about yourself when you don't or can't sustain the behavior. You may be able to act like an extrovert on an occasional basis, but it isn't natural to behave that way if, deep down, you are an introvert. It can only be done on a temporary basis, so you'll be miserable if you think you should act like an extrovert continually.

The first step towards accepting your introversion is looking at all the assumptions you hold regarding it. As you do this, you'll realize that many of your assumptions are actually wrong. Below are some examples of assumptions that you may hold.

- I'm boring if I'm not talking.
- Silence is awkward, so I should talk to avoid it.
- I don't enjoy parties, so something must be wrong with me.
- I shouldn't stay home on a Friday night.
- If I don't like talking to people because I'm shy.
- If I open my mouth, I'd better say something interesting.

You may think you have few assumptions, but you actually have thousands in each area of our life. For example, let's focus on some specific assumptions you may have when you're at a party:

- I should continue listening to this person who's talking non-stop for ages because breaking off the conversation would be rude.
- Taking a break to go for a walk during a party is weird.
- I should talk more.
- It's normal to feel guilty for talking too little.

- I should enjoy the party.
- I should have more energy.
- I should stay until the end of the party.
- I should say something interesting.
- *Everyone else having a good time, so what's my problem?

Remember that introverts account for fifty percent of the population, so you're just one of many people who doesn't enjoy parties!

∾

Action step

Use the workbook to record expectations that directly influence the way you experience your introversion. (*Section I. Owning your introversion - 2. Challenging your assumptions*)

∾

Accepting Yourself as You Are

> *Don't think of introversion as something that needs to be cured ... Spend your free time the way you like, not the way you think you're supposed to.*
>
> — SUSAN CAIN.

Do you apologize for being tall or short? What about for being a man or a woman? If you don't apologize for any of these things (and you shouldn't, you really shouldn't), then why should you apologize for being an introvert? Introversion isn't something you can turn on and off at will. It isn't a choice that you make. You need some alone time to recharge your energy, and that's not going to change. It's just how your brain works. Period.

Sure, you may be able to act like an extrovert for a few hours, but it doesn't change the fact that you need some 'alone' time to recharge your batteries. Neglecting to do that means disrespecting yourself and going against your own nature.

You aren't lacking anything

> ...*the most important thing to know about being an introvert is that there's nothing wrong with you. You're not broken because you're quiet. It's okay to stay home on a Friday night instead of going to a party. Being an introvert is a perfectly normal 'thing' to be.*
>
> — JENN GRANNEMAN, AUTHOR OF THE SECRETS LIVES OF INTROVERTS.

People often see introverts as lacking something. Some extroverts say that we lack, well, extroversion. They tell us we should talk more, go out more, and enjoy ourselves more. But people who do this are simply projecting their extroverted nature onto us.

You don't need to pretend to be extroverted to compensate for your introversion, because you aren't lacking anything. You don't need to be cured. You're not crazy, snobbish, or awkward. You don't need to become an extrovert. You just need to understand and respect yourself for who you are.

You don't owe anyone social interactions

> *I don't hate people, I just feel better when they aren't around.*
>
> — CHARLES BUKOWSKI, POET.

We often believe that we need to interact with other people. We "should" answer the phone when someone calls, we "should" say something interesting to avoid lulls in conversation, or we we "should" keep a conversation going.

Well, that's not true. Nobody has the right to force social interactions upon you. Nobody is allowed to use your precious time without your permission. You can go to a party without talking to anyone if you so choose. You can leave a conversation at any time by saying something like, "It was nice talking to you, but I've got to get going. I'll talk to you later".

Nobody is entitled to your time. Nobody can waste your limited energy unless you allow them to. Think about it this way: when an extroverted person talks to you, *they* feel good because *they* need to interact with people to recharge themselves. In a sense, you serve a purpose for them. Yet that still doesn't mean you should keep the conversation going just to be polite. It's sucking the energy out of you, and anybody who expects you to endure that endlessly is pretty selfish. Would you force an extrovert to stay home and read books because that's what energizes you? Of course not.

Remember, you don't owe anybody social interaction! Since interacting with people depletes your energy, it's important to be selective about who you talk to and for how long.

You don't have to talk

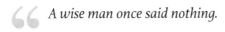 *A wise man once said nothing.*

— PROVERB.

What if I told you that you don't have to talk? Talking more doesn't make you a better human being. I used to struggle with this idea. I always felt as though I needed to say something. I assumed that I needed to be talking. As such, I felt something was wrong with me if I stayed quiet.

A few months ago, I was at a party with my work colleagues, when suddenly, something horrible happened: A lull in the general conversation. Oh no! Please, someone say something, anything! I was having a separate one-on-one conversation with someone at the time, and, when it became obvious that I wasn't joining the group conversation, someone asked me to say something. I replied, "I don't have anything to say and, to be honest, I like the silence." As you can see, introversion is no longer something I'm ashamed of. I was able to say confidently and without guilt, that I didn't have anything to say. I wouldn't have been able to do that a few years ago. Surprisingly, many people are afraid of silence. Maybe, they're afraid that they aren't interesting enough. Or maybe, they prefer to focus on the external world to avoid looking inside. In many ways, silence can be very powerful, and also very enjoyable.

You don't need to apologize for the way you feel

Remember that people can argue with what you say, but they can't argue with how you feel. How you feel is how you feel. That's it. If you feel tired and want to go home or take a break, do that. Regardless of what people say, you're responsible for your energy and how you manage it.

You don't need to feel ashamed or guilty

> What a commentary on our civilization, when being alone is considered suspect; when one has to apologize for it, make excuses, hide the fact that one practices it like a secret vice!

— ANNE MORROW LINDBERGH, AUTHOR.

It's easy to feel ashamed or guilty because you don't talk as much as you'd like or don't enjoy parties in the way you "should". You may blame yourself for not having enough energy or believing you should have more of it. You may even resent yourself for being unable to engage in small talk or be the center of attention. I once felt the same way.

The thing is, there's nothing wrong with the way you behave, nor is there anything wrong with the way extroverts behave. Your feelings and behaviors aren't strange or odd. Don't "should" yourself. Let go of your guilt and do what you truly want to do.

You don't need to be jealous of extroverts

This is a difficult one because I suspect many introverts secretly wish they were extroverts. Maybe you feel that way, too. You may envy extroverts for their ability to interact so easily with other people. You start imagining how much more popular you'd be if you were an extrovert. You may event resent them to some extent. I certainly did. In this instance, you might try hard to improve yourself to become more interesting (be it through studying, going to the gym, or honing a new skill), only to end up unnoticed and with nothing to say.

A few weeks ago, I came across one comment I found hard to forget. The comment stated that introverts couldn't be happy, as they all envied extroverts. Needless to say, I thought it was BS.

We may believe that extroverts are happy all the time, but that's not the case. Extroverts rely more on external elements (such as people) to recharge themselves. In some cases, this leads to relying on other people and other people's approval for their own happiness. They may find it difficult to spend time by themselves and may get lonely easily. Introverts, on the other hand, are often happy by themselves.

It's also important to remember that being an introvert doesn't mean you can't interact with others or be a great conversationalist. Those things are totally possible, but you'd have to be a little more strategic in how you manage your time and recharge yourself.

It's worth mentioning here, that one of the main reasons introverts may be unhappy is a general lack of understanding. We try too hard to be someone we are not. We look at ourselves through a lens that is biased towards extraversion, and then judge ourselves based on that flawed paradigm. In other words, our basic assumptions are wrong. As I said before, this creates wrong expectations and leads to unnecessary suffering.

∾

Action step

Answer the following questions using the workbook (*Section II. Owning your introversion - 3. Accepting your introversion*)

- How well do you own your introversion? Write down one negative feeling you associate with it (e.g.: feeling guilty for not talking enough, feeling tired, etc.)
- Name thing you could do or one belief you could adopt that would help you let go of that negative feeling?
- What positive feelings and emotions do you associate with your introversion? Try to write down as many as possible. (E.G. enjoying spending time at home, taking pleasure in reading a new book etc.)

∾

3

OPTIMIZING YOUR INTROVERSION

Are you generally energized throughout the day, or do you feel drained most of the time?

In this section, we'll discuss how you can redesign your day to suit your introverted personality. The first thing I'd like you to do is envision your ideal day. What would it look like? What would you be doing? How would you spend your time?

As it stands, you may have to spend time interacting with lots of people at work despite preferring small groups. Or, you might have a partner who frequently has friends over, making it difficult to relax alone.

For the moment, forget about your life as it is now. Just envision what your ideal day would look like.

~

Action step

Use the workbook to write down what your ideal day would consist of. (*Section III. Optimizing your introversion - 1. Designing your ideal day*)

- Imagine you're living the perfect life as an introvert. What does your typical day look like? What are you doing? Who are you spending your time with? How much time do you spend alone?
- What's preventing you from living like this? What's holding you back?
- What's the one thing you could do today to move you closer to the vision you have for yourself?
- Add one more thing you could do

~

Managing your energy - the key to a happy life

> *I'm very picky with whom I give my energy to. I prefer to reserve my time, intensity and spirit exclusively to those who reflect sincerity.*
>
> — Dau Voire, author.

Have you ever stayed at a party for too long only to leave feeling totally exhausted? As introverts, managing our energy is by far one of our biggest challenges. Without adequate energy, we become unable to function properly and ultimately zone out. We become grumpy, stressed out, and unhappy. Some of us even start feeling ashamed or guilty about our introverted nature.

As you can see, learning to use your energy wisely is crucial. You shouldn't allow people or situations deplete your energy. It's your responsibility to control these things. Your friends might say that you should come to a party because "it's going to be fun" or pressure you to stay longer than you'd like. This is probably well-intentioned, but the fact remains that you are the only one who knows how you feel and what you want to do. I don't like it when someone tells me what *I* should do based on what *they* want to do. I have a feeling that none of us enjoy that very much.

Telling an introvert to stay at a party when they want to go home and recharge is like telling an extrovert to go home and read when they want to socialize and increase their energy. "Come on man, you're so boring! Go home and read a book!". It sounds pretty ridiculous when you put the shoe on the other foot, doesn't it?

Finding your sweet spot

 People empty me. I have to get away to refill.

— C. BUKOWSKI, AUTHOR.

As an introvert, you have limited energy for socializing. The more you know yourself and understand your limits, the more you'll be able to avoid feeling drained at the end of the day. It's important to find your sweet spot, whether you're alone or with people.

When you're by yourself

Introverts don't mind staying home for a good while. Depending on your level of introversion, staying in for a day, weekend, or even longer might not bother you. However, spending too much time alone can make it harder to socialize on even the most basic levels. Here's a question to ask yourself: How long can I stay home before going out and handling basic interactions becomes an ordeal? Ideally, you want to avoid staying home past this point. To that end, it's good to get out on a regular basis, even if not for the expressed purpose of socializing.

Start observing how you feel when you stay home for too long, and get into the habit of leaving the house for something besides work. Sometimes, being on your own for too long can become overwhelming. Yet, even introverts need to socialize. Otherwise, we risk dwelling on negative thoughts, feeling lonely, or getting hung up on something that's bothering us.

When you're with others

How much time can you spend at a social event before running out of energy? For me, it's a couple of hours. After that point, I start feeling equal parts bored and boring. I stop enjoying myself. That's a sign that it's time for me to get out of there! For you, it may be two hours as well, but it could easily be more or less. Of course, it will also depend on the situation and how much energy you start with. Below are some factors that may impact how fast your energy is depleted:

- The loudness of the venue
- How crowded it is
- How interactive you're expected to be
- How formal the event is
- How many people you know
- How familiar you are with the venue
- Whether you can partake in activities besides talking

It's important that you learn to monitor your energy so that you can better plan your day. Once you know your sweet spot, things will become easier. Later, we'll discuss how to deal with parties as an introvert.

The importance of maintaining your space

As introverts, simply being around people can drain our energy, even when we aren't required to talk. You've probably been in situations where you're alone in a room enjoying yourself—until somebody shows up. This could happen at the gym, in the library, or at a café, to name a few examples. In any of these situations, what happened next? How did it make you feel? If you're anything like me, you probably felt mildly annoyed, anxious, or drained. I can't speak for extroverts, but my guess would be that this wouldn't be a big deal for them. They might actually get excited and strike up a conversation with the newcomer.

I hate having people around when I'm trying to enjoy something alone. When doing so, I seldom invite anyone to come with me, and if I do, they have to be an extremely close friend. I try to avoid being with others when I want to enjoy a space on my own. In that situation, friends of friends or acquaintances would be the worst people to be around, as I'd have no choice but to have some manner of conversation with them.

Have you ever made plans to get together with a friend only to have them ask if someone else can come along? How did it feel? Chances are, you were looking forward to having a deep conversation with your friend and felt it was ruined by adding a plus-one. I can totally relate to that.

Also, when you are running low on energy, note that physical contact with people, even our partner or members of our family, may be overwhelming. In some cases, you may not want anybody near you.

~

Action step

Use the workbook to optimize your level of energy. (*Section III. Optimizing your introversion - 2. Managing your energy/3. Identifying your sweet spot*)

2. Managing your energy:

- What could you do to better manage your energy?
- What is the one thing that would have the biggest positive impact on your energy level?

3. Identifying your sweet spot:

Based on your own experience, how much time can you spend at a social event before feeling the need to leave or take a break to recharge your battery?

～

Optimizing Your Life

As an introvert, you're likely to face problems in various areas of your life. In this section, I'd like to provide you with some tips to optimize your life. I'll be focusing on three different areas; your social life, career, and relationships.

Your social life

> *Introverts crave meaning so party chitchat feels like sandpaper to our psyche.*
>
> — DIANE CAMERON.

As introverts, we often have a love-hate relationship with social events. Part of us wants to go, but we can't stop thinking, "Am I going to enjoy the party?" In the end, we often wind up staying home. There's nothing wrong with staying home, of course, and parties aren't a necessity of life. That said, we all need or want to go out to make friends or network. I'm going to discuss how we can redesign our social lives to make them more "introvert-friendly".

Dealing with parties

Parties can be fun, but they can also be a nightmare for introverts if we don't handle them properly. Staying for too long can leave us completely exhausted and wishing we hadn't come. But it doesn't have to be that way. Coping with parties the introvert way will make your life easier and more enjoyable.

Deciding whether you should go

First of all, you need to decide if you actually *want* to go to the event or party. In her book *The Introvert Power*, Laurie A. Helgoe gives the following tips on deciding whether you should go.

- **How big is the party?** Usually, the bigger the party is, the more tiring it will be.
- **What is the setting?** Is it an indoor or outdoor event? Is there a lot of space or will it be crowded? How loud will it be? A beach party, for instance, will make it easier for you to take a break, go for walk, or leave when you're ready. On the other hand, an indoor party in a confined environment could quickly become overwhelming.
- **Do I know the people who will be attending?** If you know most of the people there, you'll feel more at ease. It goes without saying that not knowing anyone will likely be uncomfortable.
- **Are there any activities I can partake in that don't involve talking?** You'll typically feel more comfortable when you can do something besides talk. It makes interactions with other people much smoother. If all you can do is stand and talk, however (think cocktail parties), it'll be much more challenging.
- **Do I really want to go?** Based on your previous answers, ask yourself this: "On a scale of 1 to 10, how excited am I about this party?" In other words, will I regret not having gone? Some introverts fear that they may be missing out. So, keep that in mind when you make your decision.

Learning to say "no"

There's an extremely simple and highly effective way to handle parties you're unsure about (or don't want to go to): Just don't go! That will solve many of your problems. While it sounds easy enough, many people struggle to decline invitations and attending parties when they don't want to.

The first thing to understand is that parties aren't a must. Nobody has the right to force you to attend. It often seems as though parties are the only way to have fun. I don't know about you, but, for me, having a cup of coffee with one or two close friends can be more satisfying than going to a party. The same goes for reading a good book. Parties are overrated, and I suspect that many people (mostly introverts) don't enjoy them at all. They just pretend to. I don't know whether you enjoy parties or not, but if you don't, I would advise you to stop pretending to. Most of us spend too much time pretending or trying to fit in. We pretend to be happy, we pretend to like our jobs, we pretend our relationship is great, and so on.

Whatever you choose to do with your time is fine as long as it's authentic. There's no need to fake anything.

How to say "no"

So, you've decided to decline your friend's invitation to drink beers in a loud Irish pub on Friday night. Now, you're not sure how to tell them. Your friend thinks you're crazy and is already telling you how much fun it's going to be. "You're going to love it," he says. I wonder if he would accept your invitation to come over and read books in silence. He would just love that, right?

Think of saying no as a sign of self-respect. You should also keep in mind that, if you want extroverts to stop treating you like an extrovert, you have to embrace your introversion. If you constantly apologize for skipping things you didn't want to attend to begin with, how can you expect extroverts to change their behavior towards you? They won't be able to understand your need for solitude if you send mixed signals. Here are four tips to help you say no:

1. **Stop apologizing:** You don't need to apologize for wanting to spend your time in a way that will maximize your happiness! You don't try to keep extroverts from expressing their

extroversion. You don't try to stop them from partying all night if that's what they want to. It's their life, right? So, don't let other people do that to you. There's no need to say, "I'd like to go, but...." If you keep saying that, chances are people will continue to invite you, which might not be what you want.

2. **Own your introversion:** Instead of saying that you "need" to rest, state clearly it's what you want. "I'm looking forward to reading a great book tonight," or "I want some time to myself," or "I'm excited about staying in and relaxing." This will better convey your agenda than, "I need to rest."

3. **Be honest:** Say things as they are and embrace your introversion. The more your respect yourself and accept your introversion, the more your friends will accept it, too. Remember, many people don't understand introversion. Your real friends will be more supportive once they understand what your needs are. They'll not only support your choice to stay home, but will also help you preserve your energy during parties, which we'll cover later on. You can say something like, "You know, I'm not big on parties. I had an exhausting week and I'm looking forward to staying home and reading a great book."

4. **Offer alternatives (optional):** Sometimes you want to catch up with your friends, but not in that crowded Irish pub on Friday night. If that's the case, you can simply offer another option. You could say, "I've had an exhausting week and I'm going to recharge my batteries by reading a great book tonight. But I really want to catch up with you, so let's have a coffee this Sunday." That's a good way to show that you *do* want to see your friends, but not at a loud, overwhelming venue. You could even mention that you'll be able to have deeper conversations. This will have the advantage of helping them realize the value of your friendship.

Additional tip: It's hard to assert yourself in a society where extroversion appears to be the norm. It's even harder when many people view introversion as something that requires "fixing". Unsurprisingly, asserting yourself takes some training. Don't hesitate to practice with a friend or on your own. For instance, you could create some phrases that allow you to politely decline events you aren't interested in. Choose responses that resonate with you and rehearse them until you feel confident enough to use them in a real conversation. Check out the following examples:

- Thanks, but I really prefer small gatherings.
- Thanks, but I'm focusing on *insert project or goal here* and can't deal with distractions at the moment.
- Thanks, but I don't really go to parties, I prefer intimate gatherings with just a few friends.

Try challenging yourself to be honest while remaining polite and see what happens.

You might also want to refer to the list of affirmations at the end of this book. Feel free to use the ones that resonate with you on daily basis or create your own.

Dealing with parties the introvert way

Let's say you accept the party invitation, hopefully because you truly want to go, but start second-guessing yourself. "Am I really going to enjoy the party? Will I regret not having stayed home?" When you go to a party, there's always some level of uncertainty. Sometimes, I've gone to a party without expectations and had a great time. Other times, I've been super excited only to end up bored and disappointed. Fortunately, as introverts, there are many things we can do to maximize our chances of having a good time. Consider the following tactics:

Arriving early: Assuming it's okay with the host, arriving early to a party allows you to familiarize yourself with the environment and start interacting with a smaller pool of people. It may be easier to have one-on-one conversations or talk with a small group before everyone arrives. The venue will be quieter and less crowded.

Leaving early: As introverts, we can only spend so much time in an overly stimulating environment. There's absolutely nothing wrong with leaving early. Lately, I tend to arrive late and leave early, rarely staying more than a couple of hours. The reason for that? After a couple of hours, I don't enjoy myself anymore, so I just leave. And you should, too! There's no reason to stay after you stop having fun. When people ask me why I'm so late I reply that I had some work to do (like writing this book). When it comes to leaving, make sure you've got your escape plan ready before you go.

Bringing an extroverted friend: Remember, extroverts are not the enemy. Going to a party with an extroverted friend is a great way to help you break the ice and interact with more people than you would on your own. There are many people that I would never have met if it weren't for my extroverted friends. Your friend will do most of the talking, allowing you to preserve your precious energy.

Another perk is that they'll likely say good things about you, which is more credible than if you were to say them yourself. That may come in handy, especially if you're looking for a partner. Most of us don't like talking ourselves up, so it's nice to have a "PR" person in the form of your friend. I'm very grateful for my extroverted friends. I hope you're grateful for yours, too!

Briefing your extroverted friend(s) on your introversion: The more your friends understand your introversion, the better they'll be able to support you. You want to take a break from the party and go for a walk? No problem, your friends will understand. You want to leave early? That's okay. Although they may want you to stay, your friends will understand.

Taking regular breaks: Don't hesitate to take frequent breaks. This might mean going for a walk or going to the bathroom. You could even ask the person you're talking to if he or she wants to go for a walk with you.

For some reason, we tend to hold beliefs that prevent us from acting freely during social events. Yet in reality, you can come and go as you please, you can leave a conversation at any time, you can go for a thirty-minute walk, or you can spend fifteen minutes in the bathroom (but make sure you're not creating a queue!). You can do whatever you need or want to do. Start looking at your own assumptions. You'll probably find that you're imposing artificial limits on your behavior due to social conditioning. Consider breaking them!

Spotting other introverts in the room: You may want to "target" other introverts, as they might be easier to approach. You'll probably find them sitting by themselves or standing in the corner of the room. Try striking up a conversation with them and see where it goes. They might be easier to talk to. Although, being introverts, don't be surprised or disappointed if they say, "I'm happy on my own for the moment." (Especially if they've read this book.)

Hanging out in a strategic spot: You might choose to stand in an area where it'll be easier for you to have one-on-one or small group conversations. You could stand in a corner, near the kitchen, or in a corridor, for instance. Be on the lookout for areas that are quieter and less crowded than others.

Volunteering: This is a great way for introverts to enjoy social interactions without having to come up with something to talk about. You'll avoid those awkward moments where you don't know who to talk to or what to say. You won't have to nurse a drink all night or check your phone constantly just to have something to do (I often do this!). You could, for instance, be helping in the kitchen or taking pictures. It's generally easier for us to create connections when we're involved in an activity, such as playing sports or cooking. Because we don't actually have to approach people and come up with something to say, the conversion flows more naturally.

Focusing on others to forget ourselves: Switching your focus from yourself to others can be an effective way to reduce your anxiety. You could, for example, decide to attend a party with the objective of learning something new. You could even think of a few questions you'd like to ask someone beforehand. Using this technique, you'll be more focused on what you want to learn than you will be on your anxiety.

Setting specific goals: You can try setting tiny goals. Your goal could be to approach one group of people. Once you accomplish that tiny goal, you can go home happy. Everything that happens afterwards is just icing on the cake. Oftentimes, you may end up approaching more people than you expect. The tiny goal approach can work for all areas of your life. One of my tiny goals is to write at least 500 words per day, but today I've already completed more than 2,000. The point is, whatever you do can snowball to good effect.

Escaping from a conversation: I used to stay in conversations for hours because I erroneously believed it was rude to leave them. But here's the truth: You don't owe anybody any interaction, and nobody can drain your energy or waste your time without your consent. Now, I simply say, "It was nice speaking with you. I'll talk to you later." Or, "My friend is waiting for me, it was nice speaking with you. I'll talk to you later." Try it for yourself the next time you feel stuck in a conversation you feel has gone on for too long.

∽

Action step

Use the workbook (*Section III. Optimizing your introversion - 4a. Optimizing your social life*)

- Regarding introversion, what are your biggest struggles in that area?
- What is one small thing you could do to improve your current situation in that area?

∽

Your career

> *A good rule of thumb is that any environment that consistently leaves you feeling bad about who you are is the wrong environment.*
>
> — LAURIE HELGOE.

Do you feel totally exhausted at the end of each day? If you're working the wrong job or are in the wrong environment, you can easily feel overwhelmed. Maybe you have to make phone calls for work and you hate it. Or perhaps brainstorming sessions and endless meetings are draining all your energy. Take some time to think of the things that, if you could do less of them, would make work more enjoyable.

Using our current examples, this could mean making fewer phone calls or having a lower number of meetings. After you've thought of a few things, write them down. Similarly, think about things that would make work easier if you could do more of them. This could be prioritizing emails over phone calls. Write these things down, too.

Unfortunately, today's typical work environment isn't introvert-friendly. Open space is one of the worst things for introverts. We would rather have more private space and quiet time to focus on their work. Below are some tips to help you redesign your environment and improve your job satisfaction. Keep in mind that this list is far from exhaustive. Everyone is different, so I encourage you to come up with some specific and personal strategies that work for you.

- Have lunch alone to give yourself some "me" time.
- Use your break to go for a walk.
- Look for empty conference rooms and use them to work without interruption.
- Arrive early or stay late to carve out some time alone.
- Wear headphones to prevent people from interrupting you.

- Negotiate working from home, even if it's just one afternoon per week. It will allow you to recharge your batteries. Make sure you remain productive, as that will put you in a better position to negotiate spending more time working from home.
- Ask your boss if you can send in ideas before or after a meeting. This will show that you're motivated and present even if you can't voice your opinions during meetings. Better still, you'll have more time after the meeting to put your ideas on paper.
- Tell your colleagues that you're working on minimizing interruptions throughout the day and ask them what they need from you. It's especially important to ask this of your most distracting colleagues.
- Let your boss and co-workers know that you'd like time to settle in in the morning before talking to anyone.
- Clearly state that you'd prefer to communicate via email rather than by phone.
- Skip meetings whenever you can.
- Try setting office hours so as to create blocks of uninterrupted work time.

How to assert yourself at work

Because our introversion is natural to us, we expect those around us to think as we do, or at the very least understand us. However, introverts and extroverts think and behave very differently. Your boss and co-workers don't necessarily see you the way you'd expect them to. They may not realize how much you're contributing. It might be that you speak little because you don't realize how much you know. Or perhaps you don't like sharing your thoughts because it draws attention. People won't necessarily pick up on things like this.

Most introverts have a difficult time speaking up and putting themselves in the spotlight. People might not understand that you need time to think alone before speaking, or that not piping up during a meeting doesn't mean you aren't willing to contribute.

Check out the tips below to see how you can make your presence known.

1. Multiply one-on-one conversations: You might not be able to contribute much during meetings but, as an introvert, you're generally good at talking to people one-on-one. By creating more opportunities for one-on-one conversations, you can build deeper relationships with your colleagues. You could, for instance, invite one of them to lunch. Alternatively, you could arrive early or stay late from time to time to strike up conversations with some of your co-workers before (or after) everyone is in the workplace.

2. Offer your help: Volunteer for things that you have an interest in. Maybe you can write a newsletter or share some articles with your colleagues. Or you could suggest some useful resources. As introverts, we might not like to blow our own horns, but we typically like to help. Based on what you know regarding your colleagues or boss, what could you do to assist them? How can you help them achieve their personal goals?

3. Focus on written communication: Offer to share your thoughts and ideas after a meeting. It will give you time to think and put your thoughts on paper while demonstrating your desire to contribute.

4. Ask for help: Introverts may be reluctant to ask for help and might want to do everything on their own. Avoid giving into this urge. Asking for help is a great way to interact with your colleagues and make them feel appreciated. Many people like helping others, so it's a win-win situation.

5. Keep your boss up-to-date: You probably don't communicate with your boss as often as your extroverted co-workers do. You can compensate for this by regularly letting your boss know what you're up to.

Changing Careers

If you hate your job because it doesn't allow you to thrive as an introvert, it might be time to consider finding a new one. You might not be able to change your job right away. However, you need to ask yourself the following question: "Do I want to spend the rest of my life doing what I'm currently doing?" If not, why not prepare for your future career?

Taking time to design your ideal day will help you choose a career that suits you. You might want to ask yourself the following questions:

- What are my strengths?
- What job would allow me to leverage these strengths?
- Do I want to spend most of my time alone, in one-on-one conversations, or conversing in small groups?
- How much of my time do I want to dedicate to these activities? *If you have no clue what you'd like to do in regard to a career, check out the paragraph on finding your passion in the section V, Transcending your introversion)*

Dealing with Networking Events

Networking events may be the last thing you want to attend. Yet, they're probably not as bad as you think. Contrary to popular belief, there's no need to talk to everybody in the room or distribute business cards by the dozen. In fact, those who do this generally end up with poor results. Keep in mind that the tips mentioned for parties work well for networking events as well. Read on for nine tips on handling networking events:

1. Go deep: As an introvert, you likely crave deep, meaningful conversations. I don't see why you should ignore that craving when attending networking events. Set a small goal of building a couple of meaningful interactions rather than trying to exchange business cards with everyone in the room.

2. Set a clear goal: Before you attend a networking event, make sure you have a specific goal set. Ask yourself this: *What exactly am I trying to achieve here?* For instance, your goal could be to create two meaningful connections. Having a clear goal that you're confident you can achieve will help relieve some of the pressure. Make sure, your goal isn't too big. You can always approach more people than you set out to, but that should be optional.

3. Decide how long you'll stay: Decide beforehand how much time you plan to spend at the event. It could be as little as twenty to thirty minutes. If you wish to stay longer, feel free to do so, but don't put pressure on yourself.

4. Prepare well: As introverts, we may struggle to answer questions on the spot or come up with good questions to ask. As a result, it's best to prepare your questions ahead of time and rehearse answers to questions you might receive. Make sure the questions you ask are open-ended. It's best to avoid yes or no questions.

5. Create a simple elevator pitch: Put together a simple introduction you can use when you meet someone for the first time. Try to view this elevator pitch as your networking introduction. When you introduce yourself, make sure you mention how you help people rather than focusing solely on what you do. What value do you offer and what problem(s) do you solve? Then, you want to state who precisely you'd like to connect with. Look at your pitch as a teaser whose objective is to encourage people to ask questions that allow you to provide more details about what you do. Kathy McAfee from americasmarketingmotivator.com gives the following example[2]: "My name is __, I'm a divorce and family attorney lawyer. I help people navigate through one of the most difficult times in their lives or "I help people make smarter choices so that they can go on to have a happy life". Then, you can add, "I'm looking to connect with__".

6. Take breaks: You don't have to attend all the workshops or stay for the whole event without a respite. Take as many breaks as you need, and do it without shame!

7. The 80/20 rule: The 80/20 rule states that twenty percent of our efforts result in eighty percent of our results. The same goes for networking events. Among the networking events that you consider attending, some will offer more opportunities than others. As an introvert, why not focus on the twenty percent that are most likely to generate positive results and skip the rest?

8. Bring an extroverted friend: We discussed this in relation to parties, and it has a similar application here. Your extroverted friend will help you interact with more people and will take the edge off of things.

9. Follow-up: Make sure you follow up with the people you interact with. Consider connecting with them on social media platforms and send them a unique email based on what you discussed at the event.

Networking the introvert way

Okay, so we've talked about networking events, but who says you have to go to them, anyway? It's fine if you choose to, but if you don't want to, it's not the end of the world. They aren't a necessity. There are other ways to network that aren't nearly as stressful and exhausting as traditional networking events. Let's have a look at some of them now.

Networking online

In this modern age, we're fortunate enough to have access to this thing called "The Internet". LinkedIn would be a good place to start, but you can find many other sites or forums related to your industry that you can use for networking. You'll also find tons of groups on Facebook. For instance, I'm part of a group of writers on Facebook. I don't have to go to any events or even talk to anyone face-to-face to create connections. The possibilities are endless. So, if you hate networking events, consider focusing only on a few events, or eliminating them altogether. Focus on your online networking instead.

Leveraging your personal network

You already have a personal network, and each person in your network has his or her own personal network. Why not leverage these networks?

For example, one of your colleagues could introduce you to someone from a different industry that you'd like to learn more about. You could then have a coffee with that person.

This would be much easier than going to a networking event and hoping you'll get something out of it.

∼

Action step

Use the workbook (*Section III. Optimizing your introversion - 4b. Optimizing your career*)

- Regarding introversion, what are your biggest struggles in this area?
- What is one small thing you could do to improve your current situation in that area?

∼

Relationships

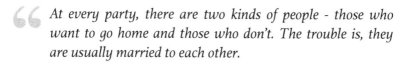
At every party, there are two kinds of people - those who want to go home and those who don't. The trouble is, they are usually married to each other.

— ANN LANDERS, FAMOUS ADVICE COLUMNIST.

Is your partner an extrovert? Do you have extroverted kids? To ensure fulfilling relationships, it's essential that extroverts understand introverts' needs (and vice-versa).

Being in a relationship with an extrovert

If you're currently in a relationship with an extrovert, chances are that he or she always wants to invite friends over and likes to go out on the weekends. This may even be a point of contention between you. You wish you could have more time for yourself and didn't have to spend so many weekends with friends or navigating through parties. On the other hand, your partner feels you're distant or antisocial. He or she may even be afraid that you don't love them when you say you need alone time.

Below are some tips that may help you improve your relationship with your parter.

1. **Make sure your partner understands what introversion is:** As an extrovert, your partner cannot experience introversion. As such, he or she may not understand why you need to spend time alone to recharge your battery. It's essential that your partner understand your needs before you try to make changes in your relationship.

You could suggest he or she read some books on introversion (like this one, for instance). The best way to encourage your partner to learn more about introversion is to learn more about extroversion yourself. Because let's face it, you don't know how it feels to be an extrovert, either. Make sure you spend some time reading some articles or books on extroversion. Additionally, ask your partner what challenges he or she encounters as an extrovert. Remember that both extroverts and introverts have challenges. This mutual understanding will make future changes (and your lives together) easier.

2. **Express your needs:** Share your needs with your partner. Maybe you wish you could have more time to yourself, or more time with just the two of you, instead of being with friends all the time. Maybe you wish you could relax on Friday night instead of having to go out with friends. Just state your needs and mention how your

partner would benefit from meeting them (for instance, it might mean you're more available or are in a better mood).

3. Listen to your partner's needs, too: Ask your partner if he or she has unmet needs. For example, your partner may believe you're a little distant and may wish that they could spend more time with you. You need to know what they want so you can help satisfy their needs, too.

4. Negotiate with your partner: Find common ground with your partner. This could mean negotiating a pattern of staying home from time to time while your partner goes out with friends. It could mean inviting friends over once a month instead of twice a month. Whatever works!

5. Give it a try: Implement a thirty-day Challenge. Once you come up with an agreement, challenge yourself to try it for thirty days. Then, see how both of you feel during that period. You might both feel significantly happier. On the other hand, some issues might arise. If this happens, you'll need to make some tweaks until you come up with a balanced solution that both of you can agree on.

6. Dealing with conflict: Introverts and extroverts have different ways of handling conflict. Extroverts prefer to confront things head-on, and often try to resolve conflicts on the spot. Introverts, on the other hand, typically loathe arguments. We also need time to process information before answering questions and resolving a conflict. To an extrovert, it may seem like their introverted partner is avoiding questions or doesn't care. In reality, the introvert simply needs time to think. Also, while extroverts may see heated conversations as necessary and even healthy, introverts may be reluctant to have such conversations because we prefer "quieter" forms of discourse.

Being in a relationship with another introvert

Being in a relationship with a fellow introvert might sound like the ideal situation. You should be able to understand each other well, and that's important in any relationship. However, being with another introvert also comes with some pitfalls that you might want to be aware of.

- Your mutual desire to avoid conflict may keep one or both of you from bringing up important issues. This, in turn, might make it difficult to move forward in your relationship. You may feel stuck in your comfort zones and unable to take things to the next level.
- You may isolate yourselves from the world. You might get so comfortable spending time alone with your partner that you begin to neglect your social life. We all need to get out and meet other people, no matter how introverted we may be.
- You may rely too heavily on your partner. If you don't have a lot of friends (or you do but don't meet with them often), you may become overly dependent on your partner for your emotional needs.

Raising an extroverted child

For introverts, raising an extroverted child can be challenging. You may feel overwhelmed and constantly tired. In this section, I'll give you some practical advice to help you better manage your energy, become an even better parent, and enhance the quality of your life.

- **Ask your extroverted partner to deal with certain activities:** If your partner is an extrovert, he or she might be able to help you deal with tasks that drain your energy. For example, your partner can handle most birthday parties and chatting with other parents. Or they can spend time engaging in extrovert-friendly activities with your child. Meanwhile, you're free to focus on chores you can do on your own such as cooking or cleaning.
- **Explain to your child that you need your "me" time:** Let your child know that you need some time to recharge your battery. Your child will have to deal with introverts at some

point in his or her life, so why not explain what introversion is?

- **Carve out some alone time every day:** Make alone time part of your daily routine.
- **Teach your child to spend time alone:** While introverts enjoy being alone, extroverts crave interaction and may have difficulty being by themselves. You could come up with activities that your child can do alone. Child development expert D. W. Winnicot states that the ability to be alone "is one of the most important signs of maturity in emotional development." It might be a good idea to teach your child to spend some time alone.
- **Reduce your exposure to activities that deplete your energy:** With an extroverted child, it makes sense to reduce any social activities that aren't directly related to your child. Instead of joining group activities, you could choose to have a coffee with a couple of friends, or spend some time alone.
- **Suggest low-key activities you can do with your child:** You could watch a movie or read books together, for instance. I don't recommend you turn your child into a TV addict, but scheduling these types of activities can give you some time to rest.

Avoiding small talk and having deeper conversations

As introverts, we crave meaningful conversation while avoiding small talk like the plague. For extroverts though, this desire to go deep so quickly can be seen as premature and even a little intimidating. In this section, we'll discuss how to go deeper and reduce chitchat without scaring anyone.

1. Be real

Being authentic from the beginning is an effective way to minimize small talk. If someone says they like something and you don't, then say so (politely, of course). If you're tired, say so. If you aren't enjoying the party, say so (nicely). By being authentic and sharing your thoughts and emotions, you give the other person permission to do the same.

2. Create hooks by sharing more about yourself

As introverts, we generally hate promoting ourselves, but it's sometimes useful to share some extra information about yourself. Instead of responding to, "How are you?" with "I'm fine, thanks," you could say, "I'm fine. I went for a walk in the park near my house this morning and the weather was perfect." Or you could say, "I'm great! I started reading a new book today, and I love it so far."

These small comments can offer additional talking point to the person you're speaking to. You could even purposely omit some details to get the other person interested. In the second example, the other person might ask, "What kind of book is it?".

The more you get into the habit of talking about yourself, the easier it will become. You can role play with some friends or try adding comments when you talk with the cashier at the supermarket, for instance.

You can also bring up some topics you're interested in and try to take control of the conversation right away. The example regarding the book you're reading would be wonderful if you love books and want the conversation to be centered around that topic. It will also give you some idea of what the other person is interested in. She may love literature, sci-fi, or books on introversion. From that point, you can further direct the conversation. Don't overdo it, though. Make sure it's a two-way conversation and the other person is interested in what you're talking about. Otherwise, they'll get bored.

3. Use open-ended questions to deepen the conversation

Asking open-ended questions is an effective way to improve conversations. The more specific they are, the better, as they'll give you a glimpse into the other person's world. Rather than asking what someone likes to do on the weekends, for instance, ask them what they did *this* weekend and what their favorite part was. That's the type of question a friend would ask, and it can seriously enhance the conversation.

Consider asking the following questions:

- Tell me more about X?
- Are you working on anything exciting these days?
- What was the best part of your weekend?
- What are you looking forward to doing this week?

Of course, this is just the tip of the iceberg. You can come up with tons of other questions!

Asking questions has a second perk: You don't have to spend as much time talking about yourself! It will lessen the pressure you might feel and make it easier to sustain the conversation without becoming anxious.

4. Assume familiarity

When talk to your friends, do you start the conversation by discussing the weather and asking them what they do for a living? Of course not! When you start a conversation with someone you don't know, assume familiarity and try talking to that person as if they were already a friend. This means skipping standard questions regarding the person's occupation, hometown, number of siblings, and so on. As you go deeper into the conversation, you'll learn the answer to those questions anyway. If you start things off on a familiar note, the standard questions will be answered much more naturally.

Consider starting the conversation by asking them how their day was or how they've been doing recently. You can then start sharing some information about yourself as we explained above. If the conversation goes nowhere, you can always ask simpler questions to get things going.

5. Try to learn something

Be curious and enter conversations with the intention of learning something about the person you're talking to. You may even want to challenge yourself to learn something specific about them. That will ensure you're as attentive as you can be. It can also keep your attention focused on them rather than yourself.

6. Steer the conversation in the direction of your choice

As introverts, we tend to be passionate about certain topics. When these topics are brought up, we suddenly get excited and can't stop talking. The good thing is that you don't necessarily have to wait for the topic to be brought up. You can introduce it yourself and steer the conversation in the direction you'd like it to go in.

You can do this in two different ways:

- **Make a list of your favorite topics:** Then, come up with some stories and questions for each topic. Discussing topics you're passionate about is a great way to see if the other person has similar interests.
- **Come back to something previously said:** You could mention something that they said earlier and ask them to tell you more about it. You could also share your personal experience or opinion on the matter.

A word of caution:

Don't go overboard. Don't hijack the conversation or ignore what the other person says. Otherwise, they'll get bored and stop talking to you.

Create situations in which small talk is unnecessary

Another way to avoid small talk is to seek out situations that don't rely on it. Let's say you decide to join a Meetup group surrounding a topic or hobby you're passionate about. Its members share the same passion or hobby, so small talk will become largely unnecessary. You can spend your time talking about your shared interests.

∾

Action step

Use the workbook (*Section III. Optimizing your introversion - 4c. Optimizing your relationships*)

- Regarding introversion, what are your biggest struggles in that area?
- What is one small thing you could do to improve your current situation in that area?

∾

4

LEVERAGING THE GIFT OF INTROVERSION

Introversion comes with a lot of benefits, none of which should be overlooked. We need more introverts who fully embrace their introversion and give their gifts to the world. As one of my friends told me, "It's time to come out of your shell, shed the fears, and share more of yourself with the world!" That's the message I'd like to share with you. It might be time for you to share more of yourself with the world, whatever that means to you.

You weren't born an introvert just so you could pretend to be an extrovert. Would you expect an elephant to climb a tree? You were born an introvert, and you're here to use all your strengths and contribute to the world as much as you can. If extroverts are the yin, introverts are the yang. If you spend most of your time trying to behave like an extrovert, the world will be out of balance for you. Nature and millions of years of evolution can't be wrong. If introverts account for around fifty percent of the population, it's because we have a role to play in our society.

Millions of introverts before you have used their talents to make the world a better place. You can, too. Now, let's go over some of the strengths that are common in introverts.

∾

Action step

Answer the following question in your workbook (*Section IV. Leveraging the gift of introversion - 1. Your biggest strength*)

According to you, what is your biggest strength as an introvert?

∾

1. Leveraging your ability to spend time alone

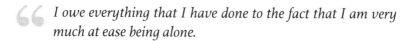 *I owe everything that I have done to the fact that I am very much at ease being alone.*

— MARILYNNE ROBINSON, NOVELIST AND ESSAYIST.

You may underestimate it, but your ability to be by yourself is one of your biggest strengths. Use this time wisely, and you'll achieve exceptional things in your life. Your ability to spend a considerable amount of time alone doesn't just allow you to think and come up with great ideas, it also enables you to get to know yourself on a deeper level. Furthermore, your 'alone time' provides opportunities to practice your craft. For extroverts, spending time alone doesn't come that easily.

2. Leveraging your propensity for deliberate practice

Practice is what creates champions. It has been shown that experts spend more time engaging in what is often referred as deliberate practice than most people do. For introverts, who would rather be left alone than work in teams, deliberate practice comes easier.

For instance, studying alone using deliberate practice has been shown to be the best predictor of skill for chess players.

Grandmasters, during their first ten years, spend 5,000 hours studying the game by themselves. This is almost five times the number of hours intermediate-level players spend studying the game. Similarly, college students who study by themselves tend to learn more than those who work in groups. The same applies to many other skills, sports, and games.

Steve Wozniak, the co-founder of Apple, credited his introversion for his creativity and success. He admitted that he would never have learned so much about computers if he hadn't been too introverted to leave the house. He spent a lot of time by himself learning about them, not because he knew all the science behind deliberate practice, but because he was an introvert with a strong passion. In his memoir, he gave the following advice, "Work alone. You're going to be best able to design revolutionary products and features if you're working on your own. Not in a committee. Not on a team." I think this is true, especially for introverts.

What exactly is deliberate practice?

In their book *Peak, Secrets from The New Science of Expertise*, Anders Ericsson and Robert Pool suggest that deliberate practice:

- Builds skills for which effective training techniques have already been established
- Takes place outside one's comfort zone, requires significant effort, and is generally not enjoyable
- Involves specific, well-defined goals
- Involves taking conscious action and requires a person's full attention
- Involves regular feedback and requires adequate responses to said feedback
- Both creates and relies upon effective mental representation (the patterns we mentioned earlier) and
- Almost always involves working on existing skills or building new ones by focusing specifically on some aspect of those skills that needs to be improved.

It's easy to see how deliberate practice can lead to better long-term results than "just putting in the work." Deliberate practice makes you work both smarter and harder by consciously focusing on improving the skills you need to reach your goal.

You might be thinking, "If deliberate practice is so great, why aren't more people using it?" There are three main reasons for that:

1. Deliberate practice must be based on existing training techniques that are effective. It works well with activities for which performance can be concretely assessed, like sports, music, or chess. Yet, it's harder to implement activities where performance is more difficult to assess (like teaching or business management).
2. It requires effort and, let's face it, most people aren't willing to go through the hassle.
3. Many people just don't know about deliberate practice and how they can use it to improve their skills.

Below are some examples of what deliberate practice is and is not.

Writing:

Typical practice:

Writing, writing, and more writing. In the words of Stephen King, "If you want to be a writer, you must do two things above all others: read a lot and write a lot." But what if it's more complex than that?

Deliberate Practice

It seems as though Benjamin Franklin felt he needed to do more than read and write a lot. He focused on improving specific skills: his writing style, vocabulary, and sense of organization.

- Writing style: He made notes on articles from *Spectator*, a high-quality newspaper, which he would use to rewrite the articles a few days later. He would then compare his version to the original and modify it accordingly.

- Vocabulary: He rewrote *Spectator* essays in verse and then in prose so that he could compare his vocabulary to that which the original article used.
- Organization: He wrote summaries of every sentence in a particular article on separate sheets of paper. He would then wait a few weeks before challenging himself to write the article in the correct order and compare his work to the original article.

Doesn't that sound like fun? And he did that consistently while holding down a full-time job!

Public speaking

Typical practice:

Practicing a certain speech again and again until your performance becomes satisfactory.

Deliberate practice:

Focusing on a specific skill or aspect of your speech that would allow you to improve your overall performance. These skills and aspects include the following:

- The tone of your voice
- Your rhythm
- The structure of your speech
- Your body language/eye contact
- The use of your space
- How you tell stories
- Your vocal projection

As you start using deliberate practice in your daily life, you'll be able to get far better results than most people. And although practice is best done alone, the benefits of deliberate practice aren't limited to solo activities. Public speaking, which involves interacting with a room full of people, requires a lot of deliberate practice. However, you can certainly become a great public speaker if you choose to. The same goes for any other skills you want to develop to create the life you want.

3. Leveraging the time you spend thinking

 It's not that I'm so smart, it's just that I stay with problems longer.

— ALBERT EINSTEIN.

As introverts, we tend to think a lot. This can be an amazing strength, as thinking is the key to problem solving, and it's been the source of many amazing ideas and inventions. An individual's ability to stay with a certain topic for a lengthy amount of time can yield some awesome things. That said, it's important to realize that this strength requires honing, otherwise it can easily turn into a weakness.

Sometimes we think so much we might even have a hard time sleeping. Our ability to think so intensely can turn from being a blessing to a curse if we're unable to control our thoughts properly.

While extroverts are often able to take action without thinking excessively, as introverts, we tend to overthink things. If we want to do something, we'll go over it so many times that just *thinking* about what it will involve drains us! *I need to take my car, then I'll have to find a place to park it. The shop will be crowded and I'll get tired. What if they don't have the right size or color. Then, when I'll go home it might be the rush hour etc.* It's almost as draining as actually *doing* what we're *thinking* about. We create all types of scenarios in our minds, which just wastes our precious energy.

Since we deplete our energy during most social interactions, this tendency to overthink might be a defense mechanism to protect our energy and avoid taking on more than we can handle. That would make sense. But overdoing it actually *wastes* our energy.

Thinking is one of the most powerful tools we have as human beings. When we begin focusing our thoughts on something that's important to us, we start unleashing our introvert power.

Since ideas can be more exciting for us than anything else, leveraging our obsession to overcome a particular challenge can allow us to achieve great results.

Tip: Each time you catch yourself overthinking, remind yourself that you can only take one step at a time. When you learn to take one step at a time and stop trying to predict the future, things can become much less overwhelming.

4. Leveraging your ability to stay focused and dig deep

As introverts, we generally prefer depth to breadth. We like to delve more deeply into specific topics, which can be used to our advantage. When we find something we're passionate about, we can get really excited and intense about it. For instance, we may be quiet for the majority of a conversation, only to talk nonstop when a topic of interest comes up. Once that happens, we'll start talking confidently and will be pretty hard to shut up. Does any of this sound familiar to you?

Nowadays, many people struggle to focus on a specific thing and instead jump from one topic to another. Even when they do have a specific goal, they jump from one diet to another, one course to the next, or this book to that book. Then they wonder why they fail to obtain the results they want. This is Shiny Object Syndrome, and it's a major problem for many people. The great thing about introversion is that, in my opinion, it makes it easier to remain focused on one goal until it's achieved. That's because introverts are less excited by novelty and external rewards. As Einstein says, "It's not that I'm so smart, it's just that I stay with problems longer." The more you train yourself to focus on one thing you love and go deeper with it, the happier you'll be. This will also increase your chances of achieving the results you want.

Now that we've covered some of the most important strengths that come with extroversion, it's time to talk about perseverance. Let's get started!

5. Leveraging your writing skills

Many introverts write better than they speak. As such, creating a habit of writing every day can make a big difference in your life. It will help you come up with great insights that will assist you in multiple areas of your life.

Keep a journal

Journaling can be helpful to anyone, but introverts may find it especially beneficial. Putting all your thoughts and ideas on paper provides two advantages:

1. It allows you to identify negative thought patterns and limiting beliefs.
2. It assists you in coming up with new ideas.

Identify negative thought patterns and limiting beliefs

As introverts, we may think too much. Yet the key question is what do we think about most? While we have thousands of thoughts every day, most of them are the same thoughts we had yesterday, last month, or even last year. Our brain is like a computer. It runs its own programs and software based on preexisting beliefs. These core beliefs are the result of repeated exposure to external stimulus, and they impact our actions on a day-to-day basis.

As you keep journaling, these core beliefs will become clear. You may constantly feel like you aren't good enough. Or you might realize that certain external events create a particular emotional reaction.

These thought patterns are self-sustaining and feed themselves. An external event triggers a core belief and generates a thought. You entertain that thought, which triggers an emotional reaction. This emotional reaction in turn reinforces your thought pattern.

Example: Someone told you your speech could have been better. You connect this event to your core belief of "I'm not good enough". It generates thoughts like "I'll never be good enough" or "I'm stupid". You identify with these thoughts and believe them, which creates an emotional reaction. This emotional reaction could be shame, frustration, or anger, among other things.

To overcome your success-limiting beliefs, you must first identify what your programming is. That is, what your thought patterns are, and what triggers them. The more you know about yourself, the better you'll be able to identify your negative patterns and stop entertaining unhelpful thoughts. You'll start seeing them as a broken record playing the same song again and again. You'll get tired of it over time and stop listening.

Each time you experience negative emotions, ask yourself the following:

- What was the trigger? - What made me shift from happiness or neutrality to a negative state of mind?
- What was the exact thought generated by that trigger? - What thought did I identify with?
- How did that make me feel? – Ashamed? Guilty? Frustrated? Angry? Sad? Something else?
- How is it serving me? - Does it serve a purpose? Is it helping me in some way?
- How often have I had similar thoughts in the past? - Is this thought like a broken record? Have you had it thousands of times before? *Use the old entries of your journal and look for similar patterns. What happened in the past?*

After the negative emotions are gone, ask yourself the following three questions:

1. What was the trigger? - What made me shift from a negative state of mind to a positive one?

2. What was my thought process? - What thought(s) created that shift?
3. How did this negative wave of emotions serve me? Did I learn something from them, or were they a waste of time and energy?

This process will help you realize that, most of the time, your negative emotions aren't helping you. That doesn't mean that they serve no purpose, however. If used correctly, they can force you to look deep inside yourself and examine the core beliefs behind these negative emotions. This, of course, allows you to change your beliefs for the better.

Coming up with new ideas

Have you ever had a great idea that you wound up forgetting? I have!

Journaling is a powerful way to capture all of your ideas in one place. It keeps you from forgetting the innovative thoughts that come your way. As introverts, we tend to be creative and enjoy thinking about various concepts. We feed on ideas. So, the more we capture, the better!

Many of your ideas won't lead to anything, but sometimes they can change your entire life. You could come up with an idea that turns into a seven-figure business. You could have an idea for a book that will become a best-seller. Or you could have an idea that will completely change the way you see the world.

If you're not journaling yet, why not get started today?

6. Leveraging your interpersonal skills

As an introvert, you may be better at talking in small groups or having one-on-one conversations. Many introverts have good listening skills that they can use to their advantage. Why not utilize your strengths and prioritize situations that better suit your personality? You'll feel increased levels of happiness, confidence, and competence, something you can't do if you're forcing yourself to act like an extrovert.

Let's just say you're looking for a boyfriend or a girlfriend. Sure, you could go out every weekend, wear your extrovert hat, and hope for the best. But that's likely to leave you tired and frustrated. It probably won't yield any results, either.

In this scenario, why not forget about loud and crowded environments and play the game on your own turf? Wouldn't it be better to be in situations where you can have the kind of conversations you're good at? Putting yourself in favorable situations will give you more opportunities to show your personality.

To this end, you could try online dating. You could also go on a double date with your friend, or meet people in cafés or libraries. You could even join Meetup groups to connect with people who share your interests. You'd be better off spending time with people who have similar passions than standing around at a party you're not enjoying.

When you hang out with people who have similar interests, it's easier to strike up conversations and small talk is unnecessary. Personally, I find it easier to interact with people when I'm talking about things I love than I do when at a cocktail party. How about you?

7. Practicing Meditation

Meditation can be particularly beneficial for introverts. Although introverts may seem calm on the surface, their inner worlds can become chaotic. Personally, a book can get me so excited I have a hard time sleeping.

On the other hand, some of us can drown in waves of negative emotions that take days to escape. I've experienced this myself. I used to criticize and even insult myself for not being the person I wanted to be. Meditation allowed me to distance myself from my thoughts and stop taking them so seriously. In times of stress, meditation has enhanced my mood and enabled me to increase my focus.

As such, I meditate for 25 minutes as part of my daily morning ritual*. I encourage you to adopt a daily meditation practice, too. You can start with as little as five minutes per day.

*If you want to create a daily morning ritual that supports your goals and increases your happiness, check out my book Wake Up Call. The book will provide you with a simple, 10-step method you can use right away to create a lasting morning ritual.

8. Leveraging your ability to persevere

Introverts tend to stay focused on a task longer than extroverts. That's because we're less dependent on external rewards and instant gratification. We don't need that extra rush of dopamine as much as extroverts do. Thus, we find it easier to think long-term and anticipate potential risks.

Perseverance often beats talent. Once we are able to maintain our levels of perseverance, over time, we will be able to accomplish things that are far beyond our imaginations. As with Einstein, our propensity to "stay longer with problems" can make a big difference.

What if you could leverage your perseverance to achieve your goals and dreams? What if you could use it to create a happier life? This could be done by learning a new skill that allows you to fire your boss and work as a freelancer. And that's just one of the many possibilities!

In this section, I'll offer a simple method to help you become significantly more adept at persevering and make the most of your introversion.

Prepare yourself mentally

Many people give up when they realize that things aren't going as well as planned. When they fail to earn tangible results after a couple of months, they jump to something else and repeat the same process, never achieving anything substantial. Whatever your goal may be, you'll face many challenging situations. In fact, you're likely to find yourself on the verge of quitting many, many times.

One of the main reasons people give up is because they start their journey with unrealistic expectations. They naively believe that things will go as planned, when we all know that they never do.

To avoid giving up too quickly, it's important to prepare for the worst even before you even start working on your goal. Ask yourself, what's the worst that could happen? What is the worst-case scenario ever? What would you do if you work on your side business for 6 months without making a single sale? What if you can't sell even one copy of that book that took you months or years to write? Considering scenarios like these will serve you well in the coming months. Make sure you visualize the situation and engage your emotions. How would you feel? Could you accept what was happening and keep pushing forward?

Let me give you a recent example related to this book. A short while ago, the computer I had been using for six years crashed and I lost all my data. Even worse, I hadn't backed up any of my data (I know, I know...). As a result, I lost the two new books I was working on along with many other files related to my business. The 25,000 words I wrote for my introversion book? Gone! Yes, I had to rewrite the book you're reading right now from scratch. What an absolute nightmare!

When I imagined the worst-case scenario, I had envisioned losing all my books on Amazon and all of the articles on my blog. However unlikely, I considered the idea of Amazon closing my account for some reason and my website being hacked. The point wasn't to come up with a realistic scenario, but to come up with the worst one to prepare myself for potential challenges ahead.

When I lost all my data and realized I would have to rewrite this book from scratch, I wasn't happy about it. However, I didn't dwell on it for days. I didn't get depressed and waste an entire week trying to change the past. I went back to work right away, because I was mentally prepared for it.

Now, imagine what would've happened if I expected things to go smoothly with little to no challenges. I would have been devastated, wouldn't I? That's why preparing for the worst is a wise thing to do. I expect to encounter many challenges in the future that are far more challenging than this one. All successful people have had to face major setbacks, and we will, too. I remember Jim Rohn discussing how he lost $250,000 because he signed a contract without reading it. At least he learned his lesson. I did, too. Now, I make sure to back up my files!

The second question is, what would make you give up? At what point would you say enough is enough? By deciding this ahead of time, you'll know that, unless you encounter that situation, you must keep going. And you can always reassess the situation. Maybe, you want to quit your job and look for another one that's more introvert-friendly. If so, what would make you give up on that goal? Will you give up after six months? One year? Two years? After ten job interviews? Twenty? Thirty?

Stick with one major goal

Having too many goals is one of the most common mistakes people make when they set goals. While having lots of short-term goals might be okay, it's usually counterproductive when it comes to long-term ones. It's far better to stick with one major goal and achieve it than to dabble in several big goals. Doing this builds your self-discipline muscles and translates to greater results over time.

You may want to use this book to improve your relationships or redesign your career. Or perhaps you want to become better at networking and deal with parties in a more "gracious" way. If you try to do everything at once, however, you'll feel overwhelmed and fail to achieve any of your goals. You'll get better results by focusing on one major goal during the next, say, thirty days.

Let's say you decide to focus first on your relationship with your partner. Once you find a satisfying balance, you can then move on the next area of your life, such as your career. Please note that this doesn't mean you shouldn't do anything to improve other areas of your life. It just means that you should focus the majority of your efforts towards your one primary goal.

Commit to Your Bullet-Proof Timeframe

The Bullet-Proof Timeframe is a concept that I came up with to help me remain patient and stick to my main goal. The idea behind it is to give yourself a period of time during which you commit to working on your major goal. The idea is to make a promise to yourself to never give up before the deadline.

My main goal is to keep writing books until I reach the deadline of my Bullet-Proof Timeframe, which is April 18th, 2020 (my 35th birthday). Each time I want to give up, I remind myself that I have time and I bring my focus back to my goal. I've had to do this dozens of times.

Below is an excerpt from my book *The One Goal*, which summarizes the main benefits of implementing a Bullet-Proof Timeframe. A Bullet-Proof Timeframe does the following:

- **It forces you to select a goal that matters to you.** Why would you care about some distant deadline two to three years from today if your goal wasn't that important?
- **It reminds you that you have time.** You can step back and look at the bigger picture. As you realize you still have time, persevering becomes less of a challenge.
- **It helps you avoid 'Shiny Object Syndrome'.** You'll stop jumping from one thing to the next if you don't get the results you expected. This is a major trap that derails many people.
- **It gives you the option to give up.** You can give yourself total permission to give up, BUT ONLY once you've reached the

deadline. Never before. Here's the mindset you want to adopt: *I can always give up when I reach my deadline, so for now I'm going to hang on and keep going.*

I hope that by now you're convinced of the benefits of setting a Bullet-Proof Timeframe. It will allow you to turbocharge your perseverance in all areas of your life.

Goal-setting crash course for introverts

Let's go over a powerful goal-setting method. This will help you as you work on redesigning your life as an introvert.

1. How to set goals

Imagine you could achieve anything you want and had no limitations whatsoever. What are the goals that, if achieved, would enable you to be the happiest introvert possible? Write down anything that comes to mind without judging it.

2. Select one goal

Select the one goal that, if achieved, would have the biggest impact on your life. Then circle it, because that will be your main goal.

3. Make it SMART

Too often, people set goals that are way too vague. When it comes to goals, the more specific, the better! So, make sure you use the SMART goal method, which is explained below. **SMART** stands for:

- Specific: What exactly do you want? What are you trying to achieve?
- Measurable: Can you assess the progress towards your goal? How will you know if you've achieved it?
- Achievable: Is it achievable? Is the timeframe realistic? Can

you put in the effort required despite other responsibilities?
- **Relevant:** Is it in line with your values? Is it exciting to you?
- **Time-bound:** Do you have a clear deadline for your goal?

4. Break down your goals

If your goal is long-term, break it down into a yearly, monthly, weekly, and even daily goal. Now, ask yourself how confident you feel about your ability to achieve your goal. On a scale of 1 to 10, you want to be at a 7 or 8. If you're below this, try extending your timeline or making your goal smaller.

5. Implement at least one daily habit to support your goal

Implement one small habit that moves you towards your goal each day. For instance, my goal involves writing books, so I make sure I write every day no matter what. My small goal is to write at least 500 words per day. That doesn't sound like much, but that's close to 200,000 words per year or 1,000,000 words in five years. That's about eight 25,000-word books a year. And I usually write more than 500 words per day! Your daily habit will help you maintain momentum and sustain long-term motivation. Furthermore, by keeping each new daily goal small, you'll also be less tempted to procrastinate. Remember to use deliberate practice with your daily habits.

Well, that's the end of this crash course. If you want to learn more about setting exciting goals, feel free to check my goal-setting book.

∽

Action step

Take the time to complete the exercises in your workbook (*Section V. Leveraging the gift of introversion - sub-sections 2 to 8*)

∽

TRANSCENDING YOUR INTROVERSION

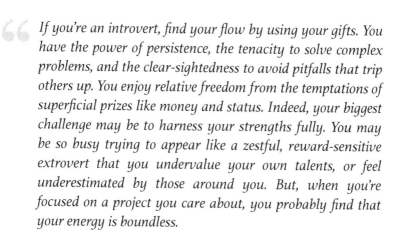

If you're an introvert, find your flow by using your gifts. You have the power of persistence, the tenacity to solve complex problems, and the clear-sightedness to avoid pitfalls that trip others up. You enjoy relative freedom from the temptations of superficial prizes like money and status. Indeed, your biggest challenge may be to harness your strengths fully. You may be so busy trying to appear like a zestful, reward-sensitive extrovert that you undervalue your own talents, or feel underestimated by those around you. But, when you're focused on a project you care about, you probably find that your energy is boundless.

— SUSAN CAIN, AUTHOR OF QUIET

You've downplayed your strengths for too many years. You've tried so hard to be an extrovert you forgot who you really are. The truth is you're as powerful as any extrovert. You have strengths most extroverts don't. You can become a leader and a source of inspiration for everyone around you. You don't need to try being the loudest person in the room to accomplish those things. Your passion is your strength, your ideas are your weapons, and your perseverance is a hidden gem waiting to be uncovered. Your written words have power, and when you speak it's because you're going to say something important. Over time, people will learn to listen to you. And sometimes, out of the blue, you'll just come up with the perfect thing to say.

Of course, your power will only come to the surface when you learn to embrace your introversion. When you fall in love with silence. When you stop apologizing for who you are. When you step out of your comfort zone, not so you can try to act like an introvert, but because it's what your mission or your calling requires you to do.

There are many myths out there that would lead you to believe introverts have limitations and can't do what others can. That, however, is total BS. If you buy into these assumptions, you'll miss out on opportunities to uncover your true potential. Do you know what Nelson Mandela, Mahatma Gandhi, and Mother Theresa had in common? Yes, they were great leaders, but there's something else: They were introverts. So how can anyone say introverts can't be leaders? How can anyone say that we need to be fixed? I don't buy either of those assumptions.

During grad school, I told a classmate of mine that I was interested in coaching. Do you know what she said? "You? You're too quiet. You never talk. How can you possibly become a coach?" Taking that thought to is logical conclusion, I should never try anything because I'm an introvert. Perhaps, I should stay home and not bother to challenge myself. I'm sorry, but that's not what introversion is about. I don't like people telling me what I can do and can't do. Do you?

When I ran a survey asking people about their biggest challenges as introverts, one of the participants wrote the following:

The biggest problem I see my fellow Introverts experiencing is accepting that they are not odd or defective because they are different in their wants and needs. Also, that they can do whatever they want to, even if it's in the Extrovert world, as long as they make time to care for themselves.

He continued:

Despite the fact I've been labeled an extreme introvert, I had a very successful career in sales which often required speaking to large groups. I loved my work, I just always made sure I set aside time to refuel after I had to be "on" for a group or client.

Did I mention that he was also a coach? Wait a minute! I thought introverts couldn't become coaches. This introversion thing is definitely more complex than I used to think!

Finding your passion

It's easy to allow yourself to become distracted and end up spending your life doing what society expects you to do. My guess is that you don't want society to tell you to live your life as an extrovert, if you did, you wouldn't be reading this book, would you?

You probably don't want society to tell you what career you should have, either. To thrive as an introvert, you must become crystal clear on what you want to do. The questions below will help you clarify your passion. I interviewed myself to give you an example of this exercise.

Who do you envy? - This is a great question and it usually shows what you are drawn to.

I envied personal development bloggers like Steve Pavlina and Leo Gura. One day, as I was watching a video from Leo Gura, everything became clear. I thought, "This is it." I realized exactly what I wanted to do: study psychology and personal development to help others. That lead me to start my blog in 2014.

What did you enjoy doing when you were a kid?

When I was a kid, perhaps seven or eight, I read books all day long. They were children's books, of course, but it was the start of my love of reading.

What activities do you volunteer for at your current job? What about your previous job?

At my first job, I volunteered to write monthly articles in Japanese regarding French culture. I also held seminars. I talked about the cultural differences between France and Japan in one of these seminars. These two examples show both my interest in writing and in psychology.

At my previous job, I wanted to figure out the best practices to encourage growth and the sharing of knowledge. I guess it's similar to what I do with my books: I gather knowledge from different sources and put them together.

What topic do you usually get excited to talk about? When was the last time you had an exciting conversation?

I enjoy talking about cultural differences, psychology, and (of course) personal development. The last time I got excited was when I talked about my online business with a friend a few days ago.

What's your way of contributing to the world? - Do you want to inspire? Entertain? Educate? Heal? Serve? Create art?

I want to help people realize what their minds are capable of achieving. I want to give them the tools they need to design their dream life.

According to you, what are your unique strengths? - What is it that only *you* can do?

One of my biggest strengths is my ability to see the best in other people—to see what they could become. I often believe in people more than they believe in themselves. My desire to help people and share information with them is another strength. When I get excited about a book or a video, I want to share it with other people. I find it frustrating when I can't share things with others. I would say my love for learning is another strength. I love consuming new information and grasping new concepts. Learning is an exhilarating, but never-ending journey.

What about you? What are you passionate about?

~

Action step

Use the workbook to answer the questions above (*Section V. Transcending your introversion - 1. Finding your passion*)

~

Supercharging your passion

Most of us don't like to be told to act like extroverts, and we'd love to be able to embrace our introversion unapologetically. But, what exactly does it mean to be an introvert? We've already seen that introversion involves the need to spend time alone to recharge our batteries. It involves becoming overstimulated in loud environments with lots of people. It also means struggling to interact with people and having a hard time thinking on the spot.

Yet introversion isn't something that limits your possibilities and imposes constraints. Sure, you need time alone to replenish your energy, but aside from that, you can do anything you want to do. I don't want you to limit your potential because of the assumptions you hold about introversion. If what you're passionate about requires you to do sales, then do it. Introverts know how to listen and ask the right questions, so, in actuality, they're often great salespeople. Do you remember what the respondent to my survey said? He wrote that he "had a very successful career in sales." He's far from being the only one. Do you remember Mr. Little? He was a terrific public speaker. You could be, too, if you so desired.

As introverts, we also have to recognize that one of our biggest strengths is our ability to become obsessed with something. When we find something we love and that gives us meaning, we can move mountains. Conversely, when we have a job that's uninspiring and neglect the things we love, breaking out of our comfort zone can become impossible.

What about you? Do you see yourself as being too intense? Are you obsessed with something? I used to believe that I was too obsessive and I needed more balance in my life. The truth is I've been this way for most of my life. First, it started with books. When I was little, I would spend most of my days reading books in my bedroom. Then, I start playing video games. After that, I became obsessed with table tennis. In high-school, I would train every day before and after school. Then, there was online gaming. I would sometimes play until 4am during the weekends. Needless to say, my mother was worried about me. In college, I became obsessed with studying. Finally, I became obsessed with personal development.

While obsession can be a negative thing, I've recently started looking at it in a different light. I thought, "What if my obsession is actually my biggest strength?" I wondered what would happen if I decided to embrace it rather than repress it. I pondered what would happen if I focused entirely on something I'm passionate about.

Your personal story may be different from mine, but you might be able to relate to it to a certain degree. The point is that your desire to delve deeper and your need to find meaning in what you do can be an extremely powerful driver. In fact, it could very well be one of your greatest strengths as an introvert.

For these reasons, I think escaping from your comfort zone to make your dreams a reality is part of introversion. It's part of giving your gift to the world. I don't see it as trying to be an extrovert, but that's just my opinion. You don't have to agree with me. In the end, the most important thing is that you live a happy life as an introvert and leave this world with no regrets! I think we can agree on that., can't we?

Once you're grounded in your introversion and focused on your mission, you can become a great example to others. People will envy your self-discipline, focus and passion. Introversion is part of who you are, so embrace it. Embody it. It's part of what makes you 'you,' and nothing in the world can change that.

∼

Action step

Answer the questions in your workbook (*Section V. Transcending your introversion. - 2. Supercharging your passion*)

- What skills must you develop to supercharge your passion?
- What things beyond your comfort zone will you need to do to live a meaningful life?

∼

Supercharging your ideas

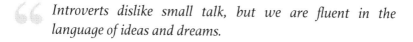

Introverts dislike small talk, but we are fluent in the language of ideas and dreams.

— MICHAELA CHUNG.

As introverts, we love ideas. Ideas are what excite us and make us come alive. Chances are, you have a lot of ideas you've never shared with anybody else. You may be reading one book after another, accumulating a vast amount of knowledge. Or you may spend a lot of time thinking and coming up with new things.

Writing down insights in a journal, or spending time to think on your own are effective ways to generate more ideas. Of course, you may not be big on sharing your ideas with the world. Yet, that's part of supercharging our introversion and sharing our gifts to the world. To this end, I believe it's our responsibility to put our ideas out there. As the late Wayne Dyer said, "Don't die with the music still in you." If you were to die today, what ideas and projects would the world miss out on because you didn't dare to share them? I don't want to die with the music still in me. I want to play my music and see how it impacts the world around me. Don't you?

You can share your ideas verbally or through writing. It might be through art or through your business. Whatever the means may be, communicate them to the best of your ability. That's the way to supercharge your introversion. That's how you can share your gifts with the world.

~

Action step

Answer the questions in your workbook (*Section V. Transcending your introversion. - 3. Supercharging your ideas*)

- Are you capturing your ideas in an effective way? If not, what could you do to capture them more efficiently?
- Are you sharing your ideas and putting them out there? If not, what could you do to share your ideas and make a bigger contribution to the world?

~

Understanding introversion is not a label to wear

Once we start understanding introversion, we may feel like we don't need to make an effort anymore. We think that, because we're introverted, we should stop interacting with people, stay away from public speaking, and stay home as much as possible. None of these things are true, however.

Yet it's easy to fall for that and live by our own definition of introversion. As we mentioned earlier, many of us hold false assumptions that don't serve us well. When we label ourselves as introverts, we risk missing out on opportunities for growth by clinging on to beliefs that aren't necessarily true.

I don't believe it's realistic to think we can live according to our vision of introversion all the time. Nor is it in our best interest. Just as extroverts may feel lonely when they have no one to go out with, we may find ourselves overwhelmed at parties we didn't plan, or want, to attend. It would be misleading to say that extroverts have it easy and live perfectly balanced lives, while introverts are a mess. We all have our challenges. Many introverts suffer loneliness, wishing they could interact with people more often. We all have to deal with some level of discomfort.

I can already hear you screaming, "Why are you saying I should act like an extrovert!" Don't worry, that's not what I'm saying. It's up to you whether you want to learn public speaking or talk to a lot of people at a party. It doesn't mean you aren't an introvert, it just means you're going beyond your comfort zone to achieve something you want. I've found that, when I have a strong sense of purpose, I'm more willing to do things that, as an introvert, I normally wouldn't want to do.

For instance, I'm not big on sharing information about myself, but I do it in my books and videos. I've also been a member of Toastmasters, a public speaking organization, for three years. I discovered that delivering speeches and shooting videos isn't that bad. I actually started enjoying both, primarily because I have a bigger purpose. If I need to shoot videos or do seminars to reach more people, I'll do just that. I just won't do it all the time. And I would be reluctant to do it for a cause I'm less than passionate about.

The final point I'd like to make is that it's easy to mistake shyness for introversion, or even fear for introversion. Thus, I would encourage you to try things out and test your own boundaries. You may end up enjoying activities that you would never thought you'd like.

∾

Action step

Answer the question below using your workbook (*Section V. Transcending your introversion. - 4. Introversion is not a label to wear*)

Could labeling yourself as an introvert (using your own definition of introversion) potentially harm your growth and fulfillment in life? If so, how?

∿

Becoming a leader

❝ *In a gentle way, you can shake the world.*

— Mahatma Gandhi.

Anyone can be a leader. Being a leader isn't reserved for extroverts. If you have any kind of impact on those around you, you're already a leader. If you have control over your own life, you have what it takes to be a leader. After all, isn't a leader someone who ushers others along a certain path? And how can you lead people life they aren't inspired by your actions and the control you have over your life?

Indeed, being a leader starts from within. Your ability to control your mind, body, and attitude determines your level of influence. That's not something reserved for extroverts. Many great leaders have been introverts. They weren't the loudest in the room, but their actions spoke louder than their words. To paraphrase Gandhi, they were embodying the change they wanted to see in the world.

Your ability to lead people and inspire them to change depends on whether they see you as a role model. Do you want to know if you're a leader? Ask yourself, "How have I impacted people around me?" Have you influenced your partner, kids, friends, or colleagues in a positive way? Do people look at you as a role model?

Introverts can be great leaders. We can even outperform extroverts in certain situations. A 2010 study conducted by the Harvard Business Review showed that, when leading extroverts, introvert were more effective leaders than extroverts. The opposite was also true. Extroverted leaders outperformed introverted ones when it came to leading introverts.

The bottom line is that, as an introvert, you can be as competent a leader as any extrovert.

Some successful introverts

Now, let's have a look at some highly successful introverts. You'll see that some of the most successful people on earth are actually introverts. Their introversion may even be one of the reasons they reached the pinnacle of success.

Bill Gates - Fiercely un-shy

The founder of Microsoft can be very quiet, but he becomes very outspoken when it comes to his passion, which is business. I believe this is true for many introverts. Our passion can energize us and give us tremendous power.

Gates said the following in one of his speeches:

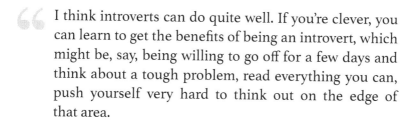

> I think introverts can do quite well. If you're clever, you can learn to get the benefits of being an introvert, which might be, say, being willing to go off for a few days and think about a tough problem, read everything you can, push yourself very hard to think out on the edge of that area.

Warren Buffet - Calculated risks

This successful investor is an introvert. His ability to take calculated risks rather than letting excitement get in his way is probably part of his success. While many investors live near Wall Street, he lives in a modest house in Omaha, far away from the hype.

Mark Zuckerberg - Depth over breadth

The founder of Facebook is an introvert. He may not have as many connections as extroverted CEOs, but his ability to create genuine connections and persuade startup founders to join his company is definitely a strength. As an introvert, his desire to prioritize depth over breadth seems to work in his favor.

Fast Company's article "Facebook's Plan to Own Your Phone," had this to say:

> The fact that Zuckerberg can more often than not persuade startup founders to join the company and work with him is a vote for the glass-half-full perspective. 'What I found compelling was Mark's commitment to spending a lot of time with us.'
>
> — BRENDAN IRIBE, OCULUS CEO

Cristina Aguilera - Intensity

You would expect the pop star Christina Aguilera to be an extrovert, but she is actually an introvert. She revealed to *Marie Claire* that she had always been intense and introverted. She felt like an outsider her whole life.

This goes to show that nothing prevents introverts from becoming great entertainers. Putting on a show or playing a certain character can actually be very enjoyable for us. It gives us opportunities to express ourselves without interruption. How cool is that? That's why I sometimes enjoy public speaking. I know people have to listen to me, and there's something nice about that.

Emma Watson - The non-party girl

In a world that expects people to behave like extroverts, this actress once felt like something was wrong with her. She didn't want to go out and "have fun" like her friends. She mentioned that learning about introversion was a relief and very empowering.

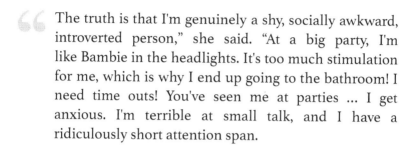

The truth is that I'm genuinely a shy, socially awkward, introverted person," she said. "At a big party, I'm like Bambie in the headlights. It's too much stimulation for me, which is why I end up going to the bathroom! I need time outs! You've seen me at parties ... I get anxious. I'm terrible at small talk, and I have a ridiculously short attention span.

Mahatma Gandhi – Thoughtful

Speaking at length was a struggle for Gandhi throughout his life. Like most introverts, he needed time to prepare his speeches. He carefully chose his words. Yet that thoughtfulness spared him many problems.

As he said himself:

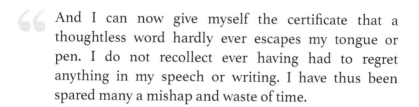

And I can now give myself the certificate that a thoughtless word hardly ever escapes my tongue or pen. I do not recollect ever having had to regret anything in my speech or writing. I have thus been spared many a mishap and waste of time.

Albert Einstein - Staying with problems longer

Einstein, like most introverts, did his best thinking while alone. His ability to spend time alone and stay focus on a problem for an extensive period of time may have contributed to his discoveries. Focusing on a specific goal for years without being distracted has been shown to be an extremely important factor for success.

"It's not that I'm so smart," he once said. "It's just that I stay with problems longer."

In the eyes of society, you may not end up as successful as the people I've mentioned. Yet I have no doubt that you have extraordinary room for growth. Embracing your introversion rather than seeing it as a handicap will allow you to make a difference in other people's lives. The question is, how will you do it? Will it be through your intensity? Your perseverance? Your thoughtfulness? Your obsession with your passion? Your ideas? That's what you'll have to figure out!

~

Action step

Answer the questions below using your workbook (*Section V. Transcending your introversion. - 5. Becoming a leader*)

- What would you say your biggest strength is?
  (Thoughtfulness, perseverance, intensity etc.)
- What is one strength, that, if further developed, would make the biggest difference in your life?

~

CONCLUSION

I'd like to thank for buying this book. In an extroverted world, being an introvert can sometimes be challenging. It's my sincere hope that this book helps you reassess the way you see your introversion.

Introversion is not something to be ashamed of, but rather something to celebrate. We should never have to apologize for being an introvert. We may encounter resistance from people who want to drag us to the next exciting party. However, we should remain true to ourselves and communicate our needs and desires politely (but firmly).

Remember that introverts aren't a minority. It's our frequent silence and the difficulty we have in accepting our true nature that makes it seem that way. We can be easily overlooked, and many of us try to pretend to be extroverted. It's only by asserting ourselves and embracing our introversion that the extroverts around us will start to understand it.

If that happens, introversion might become mainstream someday. The workplace will be redesigned with introverted employees in mind, and the way employees interact within the company will be totally transformed. The quality of our relationships with friends and family will improve. We'll be encouraged to leverage our strengths for society's greater good, and the definition of "having fun" will expand. In short, the world will give equal consideration to introverts and extroverts.

But for now, we must proudly live our lives as introverts. We have to remember that we're more than just a label. Once we set our minds to something, we have the power to accomplish exceptional things. With an inspiring enough vision, we can overcome almost any obstacle that stands in our way.

In many cases, the limits we imposed on ourselves are nothing more than ideas in our mind. Remember than Gandhi, Mother Theresa, and Nelson Mandela were introverts like you and I are. While you may not be the next Gandhi, you can be a better you. A 'you' who isn't afraid of your introverted nature, a 'you' that will do whatever you can to give your gifts to the world and be as happy as possible.

If this book helps you in any way, please don't hesitate to let me know and share your story. Also, please feel let me know if you have any feedback. And, if you enjoy the book, don't forget to leave me a review on Amazon. It would mean so much to me!

If you have any questions, contact me at

thibaut.meurisse@gmail.com.

I'll get back to you as soon as possible.

I'm looking forward to hearing from you very soon!

Warm regards,

Thibaut Meurisse.

Founder of whatispersonaldevelopment.org

Affirmations for introverts

Feel free to repeat these affirmations on a daily basis or to create your own affirmations.

Parties

- During parties, I give myself complete freedom to behave and act according to my mood
- I release all expectations and let go of any pressure I put on myself
- I allow myself to enjoy parties without any expectations or any desire for specific outcomes
- Reading a book is as valuable as going to a party
- I leave parties when I don't enjoy it and I'm perfectly fine with it
- I take breaks whenever I want without apologies

Silence

- I give myself permission to say nothing. That's my way to celebrate my introverted nature
- My silence gives space to myself and to others to simply be.
- I choose to be silent whenever I feel like it.
- I love silence.
- Being silent is doing something
- I don't owe anybody any interaction

Self-respect

- I put my own needs first.
- I show respect to myself by saying "no"
- I know what I need better than anyone else
- Staying home is doing something
- As an introvert there is nothing I should or shouldn't do.
- Managing my energy is respecting myself

Managing energy

- Managing my energy is a favor to myself and everyone around me.
- I manage my energy so that I can give my best gift to the world
- Managing my energy is respecting myself

Accepting introversion and extroversion

- I let go of any negative emotions towards extroverts
- I love myself. I love extroverts
- I embrace my introversion and respect other people's extroversion
- Both introversion and extroversion are needed in this world
- I have my challenges, extroverts have theirs.
- By accepting other people's extroversion, I accept my own introversion

Living up to my potential

- As an introvert I can achieve anything I set my mind to. I just have to manage my energy well.
- I'm more than my introversion and can transcend it whenever necessary
- I can wear the extrovert hat whenever I want and I'm fine with it.
- When I'm passionate I can do anything
- I refuse to be less than I can be

What do you think?

I want to hear from you! Your thoughts and comments are important to me. If you enjoyed this book or found it useful **I'd be very grateful if you'd post a short review on Amazon.** Your support really does make a difference. I read all the reviews personally so that I can get your feedback and make this book even better.

Thanks again for your support!

Other books by the author:

Goal Setting: The Ultimate Guide to Achieving Life-Changing Goals (Free Workbook Included)

The One Goal: Master the Art of Goal Setting, Win Your Inner Battles, and Achieve Exceptional Results (Free Workbook Included)

Habits That Stick: The Ultimate Guide to Building Habits That Stick Once and For All (Free Workbook Included)

Wake Up Call: How To Take Control Of Your Morning And Transform Your Life (Free Workbook Included)

Productivity Beast: An Unconventional Guide to Getting Things Done (Free Workbook Included)

ABOUT THE AUTHOR

THIBAUT MEURISSE Thibaut Meurisse is a personal development blogger, author, and founder of whatispersonaldevelopment.org.

He has been featured on major personal development websites such as Lifehack, TinyBuddha, PickTheBrain, stevenaitchison, guidedmind, DumbLittleMan or FinerMinds.

Obsessed with self-improvement and fascinated by the power of the brain, his personal mission is to help people realize their full potential and reach higher levels of fulfillment and consciousness.

In love with foreign languages, he is French, writes in English, and has been living in Japan for the past 7 years.

You can connect with him on his Facebook page

https://www.facebook.com/whatispersonaldevelopment.org

Learn more about Thibaut at

http://amazon.com/author/thibautmeurisse

Bibliography

On introversion

- *Quiet: The Power of Introverts in a World That Can't Stop Talking*, Susan Cain
- *Introvert Power: Why Your Inner Life is Your Hidden Strength*, Laurie A Helgoe
- *The Introvert Advantage: How Quiet People Can Thrive in an Extrovert World*, Mari Olsen Laney
- *Introverts in Love: The Quiet Way to Happily Ever After*, Sophia Dembling
- *The Introvert's Way: Living a Quiet Life in a Noisy World*, Sophia Dembling

On relationships

- *The 5 Love Languages: The Secret to Love That Lasts*, Gary Chapman

On perseverance

- *Grit: The Power of Passion and Perseverance*, Angela Duckworth
- *Peak: Secrets From the New Science of Expertise*, Anders Ericsson and Robert Pool
- *Talent is Overrated: What Really Separates World-Class Performers from Everybody Else*, Geoff Colvin

On goal setting

- *Goals!: How to Get Everything You Want Faster Than You Ever Thought Possible*, Brian Tracy
- *Wishcraft: How to Get What You Really Want*, Barbara Sher, Annie Gottlieb

GOAL SETTING BOOK PREVIEW

Introduction

Mr. Rohn, let me see your current list of goals. I've had a lot of experience and I've been out here for a while, so let's go over them and maybe I can really give you some good ideas." And I said, "I don't have a list." He said, " Well, if you don't have a list of your goals, I can guess your bank balance within a few hundred dollars." And he did.

— JIM ROHN, THE JIM ROHN GUIDE TO GOAL SETTING

I would like to thank you for downloading this e-book. In doing so, you have already shown your commitment to bettering your life by setting goals that truly excite you. You have joined those who have made the decision to take more control over their lives and give less power to circumstances. It's important to think about what where you want to be, whether it's one month, six months, one year, five years or even a decade or more from now. Taking the time to identify the goals you wish to accomplish is the best way to make sure that you're going into the right direction. It will also keep you from pursuing goals that won't fulfill you.

Deciding to set goals is probably one of the most important decisions you can make, but most people don't set clear goals in their life. It's almost as if they believe they have no control over their life. As such, they wander through life heavily influenced by the circumstances and people around them. They give their power away to their environments instead of using it to create the lives they desire. They achieve far les than they would if they took the time to plan their lives and set specific goals.

Keep in mind, however, that having goals in and of itself is not enough. In fact, having goals that are unclear or out of alignment with what you want can be almost as bad as having none at all. Unfortunately, many goal setters spend years in dogged pursuit of a particular goal only to achieve it and realize that isn't what they genuinely wanted. This e-book will help you avoid that. Setting specific goals is one of the best decisions I've made in my life and the information within this book will give you an opportunity to do the same.

I first created a list of goals back in September of 2014 while in the process of building my website. Looking back, I often wonder why I'd never done it before and why I never learned about it in school. Setting goals is par for the course when it comes to personal development, however.

I believe that we all have the potential to accomplish great things in life. However, many of us never learned to tap into our intrinsic ability to self-motivate. We spend our childhoods studying to get good grades and trying to fit in in an attempt to please our parents, teachers, and peers. We then spend our adulthoods working for money and other external motivators. Our tendency to rely upon outside motivators is ironic considering how ineffective they are. Studies show that extrinsic motivators such as money are less efficient than intrinsic motivators like autonomy, self-mastery, or finding purpose. The carrot and stick approach is still in frequent use these days, but it's far from ideal. The reality is that intrinsic motivation yields better results and provides a greater sense of fulfillment than extrinsic motivation does.

Fortunately, learning to set the right goals will help you tap into your intrinsic motivation and allow you to uncover your hidden potential. This book is intended to help you figure out what you want to achieve and the kind of life you wish to create for yourself. I want you to set goals that inspire you, stir your soul, and make you want to jump out of bed every morning. Goal setting might seem intimidating, but it's more than worth it!

What you will learn in this book:

Within this book, you'll find a comprehensive method to achieve your goals. You won't just learn how to set goals effectively, you'll also learn to think better thoughts, overcome obstacles, and persevere until you reach your goal.

This Book Will:

1) Give you the opportunity to discover and set goals that genuinely matter to you

2) Help you set short-term, mid-term, and long-term goals in multiple areas of your life.

3) Help you realize your potential and achieve more than you thought possible.

4) Provide you with an effective strategy to achieve the goals you set.

5) Enable you to avoid the obstacles you will encounter while working towards your goals.

This book is full of valuable information, but remember that how much you get out of it is largely dependent upon how committed you are to implementing it. The ball is in your court!

I. Why goal setting is important

People without goals are doomed to work forever for people who do have goals.

— BRIAN TRACY.

Setting goals gives direction to your subconscious mind

Your automatic creative mechanism is teleological. That is, it operates in terms of goals and end results. Once you give it a definite goal to achieve, you can depend upon its automatic guidance system to take you to that goal much better than "you" ever could by conscious thought. "You" supply the goal by thinking in terms of end results. Your automatic mechanism them supplies the means whereby.

— MAXWELL MALTZ.

Did you know your subconscious mind could help you achieve your goal? Setting goals gives you a direction in life, but vague goals like making more money or being happy won't lead to a fulfilling life. Your subconscious mind is like a powerful machine, and understanding how it works is a big part of successful goal setting. Hypnotherapist Joseph Clough compares it to a GPS whereas Maxwell Maltz, author of Psycho-Cybernetics, calls it a mechanical goal-seeking device. If you put an address into your GPS, it will do whatever it can to reach your destination. The subconscious mind behaves similarly. Have you ever learned a new word only to find yourself hearing it everywhere you go? That's an example of your brain "priming". In other words, it's scanning your environment for all information relevant to the word, phrase, or details you've given it. As such, setting clear goals gives you a greater chance of accomplishing them. It sends a strong signal to your subconscious mind, which allows it to unleash its focusing power and look for any opportunities to achieve the goal. We talk more about the importance of specific goals later.

Setting goals empowers you

If you don't design your own life plan, chances are you'll fall into someone else's plan. And guess what they have planned for you? Not much.

— JIM ROHN.

Are you the one choosing your goals? Or are others choosing them for you? When you start setting intentions, you stop giving away your power.

When you start setting objectives in all the main areas of your life such as finances, relationships, career, and health, you stop giving power away and start empowering yourself. You make a conscious choice to become the creator of your life and begin to take responsibility in every aspect of your life.

Imagine the difference it would make in your life if you were to take the time to figure out your goals for the future. If you knew how much you wanted to earn in five years, how long you wanted to live, and where you'd like to be in twenty years, what would you do differently?

Setting goals increases self-esteem

High self-esteem seeks the challenge and stimulation of worthwhile and demanding goals. Reaching such goals nurtures good self-esteem. Low self-esteem seeks the safety of the familiar and undemanding. Confining oneself to the familiar and undemanding serves to weaken self-esteem.

— NATHANIEL BRANDEN.

Did you know that you could increase your self-esteem by setting clear goals? It's worth mentioning that having clear goals and achieving them builds and reinforces our self-esteem. In fact, Nathaniel Branden (author of *The Six Pillars Of Self-Esteem*) states that part of our self-esteem comes from a "disposition to experience ourselves as competent to cope with life's challenges". With every achievement we accomplish, we feel better equipped to deal with other goals and life challenges. In *The Pursuit of Happiness* David G. Myers shows that high self-esteem is one of the best predictors of personal happiness. Consistently accomplishing the goals you set is one of the most efficient ways to build self-esteem.

Goal setting changes your reality

The value of goals is not in the future they describe, but the change in perception of reality they foster

— DAVID ALLEN, GETTING THINGS DONE

Setting goals is a valuable process on its own, regardless of whether or not you'll achieve them. You're probably wondering why that's the case. Well, there are several reasons. Goal setting helps you think about your future, gives you an opportunity to reflect on your values, and helps you discover what matters most. It will bring clarity and allow you to see the bigger picture of your life. It doesn't get much more valuable than that.

Setting goals will also allow you to reconstruct your reality and realize that dreams you previously thought unattainable are in fact achievable. It all starts with identifying your real desires, no matter how ambitious they are. In so doing, you'll begin the process of overcoming your limiting beliefs. Limiting beliefs stem from past experiences and make it harder to get the life you want. You'll soon realize how restrictive limiting beliefs are and just how many of them stem from repetitive messages received from family, friends, and the media.

Lastly, goal setting will give you the opportunity to assess your current situation and close the gap between where you are and where you want to be.

Setting goals is good for your health

Use goals to live longer. No medicine in the world – and your physician will bear this out – is as powerful in bringing about life as is the desire to do something.

— David J. Schwartz, The Magic Of Thinking Big.

Dan Buettner, the author of *The Blue Zone: Lessons for Living Longer From the People Who've Lived The Longest*, identified 10 characteristics shared by those who live to 100. He identified "having a life purpose" as one of them. Setting goals that fully excite you is one of the best medicines and will work wonders for your health. An alarming number of people die within a few years of retirement. I believe this is partly because they no longer have exciting goals to motivate them, something that is especially likely for those who heavily identified with their job. What about you? Have you found goals that will motivate you well into old age?

How to set goals

The key to goal setting is for you to think on paper. Successful men and women think with a pen in their hands; unsuccessful people do not.

— BRIAN TRACY.

You can learn more at:

http://amazon.com/author/thibautmeurisse

THE THRIVING INTROVERT — WORKBOOK

Assessing your introversion

Before we get started, I'd like you to take a quick survey to give you an idea of your level of introversion. On a scale of 1 to 10, how true are the following statements? Write down a number next to each statement.

1. I hate small talk, but I enjoy deep conversations.
2. I get tired if I stay at a party for too long.
3. I feel like everything I say should be meaningful and often refrain from talking for this reason.
4. I prefer one-on-one or small group conversations over talking in large groups.
5. I need to spend time alone to recharge my battery.
6. I think before I speak.
7. I have difficulty thinking when in a group. I think best when I'm on my own.
8. I usually listen more than I talk.
9. I dislike interruptions.
10. I hate conflict.

If you agree with most of these statement and have a high score, you are definitely an introvert.

I. Understanding introversion

In this section, we'll deepen your understanding of introversion and take a closer look at your relationship with it.

1. Your personal definition of introversion

Write down your personal definition of introversion in the space below.

_____

_____

_____

2. Your relationship with your introversion

Write down how your introversion makes you feel (ex: I feel ashamed, I feel frustrated, I feel proud, etc.)

_____

_____

_____

3. Introversion vs. shyness

To better thrive as an introvert, it's important to differentiate between introversion and shyness.

Imagine various interactions in your life and ask yourself: Why aren't I talking? Write down your reasons below. Then write whether the reason is based on shyness (feeling scared and uncomfortable) or introversion (feeling too low on energy). For shyness write "S", for introversion write "I".

-

-

-

-

-

-

-

If you identified yourself as shy, what is one small thing you could do to start overcoming your shyness?

_____

_____

_____

4. Your expectations regarding this book

Write down what you want to get out of this book. It will help you stay focused throughout the reading process. What is your goal?

(Ex: improving my relationship with my partner, becoming better at networking, accepting my introversion, etc.)

_____

_____

_____

II. Owning your introversion

I. Your biggest challenge

What is the biggest challenge you face as an introvert? Write it down in the space provided.

_____

_____

_____

Write down all the things you could do to overcome that challenge:

-

-

-

-

-

-

-

-

-

-

-

What is the one thing that would have the biggest positive impact on your life?

_____

_____

_____

2. Challenging your assumptions

What are some assumptions that you have? By this I mean things you believe you should do but that may go against your introverted nature.

-

-

-

-

-

3. Accepting your introversion

How well do you own your introversion? Write down one negative feeling you associate with it (ex: feeling guilty for not talking enough, feeling tired, feeling uninteresting, etc.)

My negative feeling:

_____

_____

_____

Write down one thing you could do or one belief you could adopt that would help you let go of that negative feeling.

Now, write down all the positive feelings and emotions that you associate with your introversion. Try to write down as many as possible.

Ex: enjoying spending time at home, taking pleasure in reading a new book, feeling at peace when you go for a walk in nature, etc.

-

-

-

-

-

-

-

III. Optimizing Your Introversion

1. Designing your ideal day

Imagine you're living the perfect life as an introvert. What does your typical day look like? What are you doing? Who are you spending your time with? How much time do you spend alone?

Write down your ideal day below.

My ideal day:

_____

_____

_____

_____

_____

_____

What's preventing you from living like this? What's holding you back?

_____

_____

_____

What's one thing you could do today that would move you closer to the vision you have for yourself?

_____

_____

_____

What's one more thing you could do?

_____

_____

_____

2. Managing your energy

As an introvert, managing your energy is one of the most important things you can do to live a happier life.

Write down all the things you could do to better manage your energy.

-

-

-

-

-

-

-

-

-

What is the one thing that would have the biggest positive impact on your energy level?

My one thing:

_____

_____

_____

3. Identifying your sweet spot

Based on your own experience, how much time can you spend at a social event before feeling the need to leave or take a break to recharge your battery?

_____

_____

_____

4. Optimizing your life

a. Optimizing your social life

Regarding introversion, what are your biggest struggles in that area?

-

-

-

What is one small thing you could do to improve your current situation in that area?

My one thing:

b. Optimizing your career

Regarding introversion, what are your biggest struggles in that area?

-

-

-

-

What is one small thing you could do to improve your current situation in that area?

My one thing:

c. Optimization your relationships

Regarding introversion, what are your biggest struggles in that area?

-

-

-

-

What is one small thing you could do to improve your current situation in that area?

My one thing:

IV. Leveraging the gift of introversion

1. Your biggest strength

According to you, what is your biggest strength as an introvert?

_____

_____

_____

2. Leveraging deliberate practice

How can you use the time you spend alone to improve the skills you need to achieve your goals?

_____

_____

_____

3. Leveraging the time you spend thinking

We all operate with certain thought patterns that determine most of our actions and feelings. As an introvert, your ability to think and come up with new ideas is a great asset. However, if you don't know how to use your thoughts constructively, they can wreak havoc on your emotional well-being.

What are some negative thoughts that you experience on a regular basis? What are they trying to tell you?

_____

_____

_____

_____

_____

_____

4. Leveraging your ability to stay focus and dig deep

What is the one thing that would have the biggest positive impact on your life if you were to stick with it long-term?

_____

_____

_____

5. Leveraging your writing skills

If it resonates with you, keep a journal and write down your thoughts and ideas.

6. Leveraging your interpersonal skills

How can you leverage your interpersonal skills? Examples could include increasing one-on-one conversations at work or changing your career.

_____

_____

_____

7. Practicing Meditation

If you wish to meditate, write down your new daily meditation practice. How long will you meditate each day, for instance?

_____

_____

_____

8. Leveraging your ability to persevere

Sticking with one goal

What is one goal that, if achieved, would have the biggest impact on your happiness? You can use your answer to the previous question.

My goal:

_____

_____

_____

Preparing yourself mentally

- What is the worst thing that could happen as you work on your goal?

_____

_____

_____

- What would you do if it happens? Visualize the situation and how you would feel.

_____

_____

_____

- What would make you give up one your goal? At what point would you decide to quit?

_____

_____

_____

Committing to your Bullet-Proof Timeline

Write down your Bullet-Proof Timeline (the deadline before which you won't allow yourself to give up):

My Bullet-Proof Timeline: ___/___/20___

Goal-setting crash course for introverts

Let's go over a powerful goal-setting method. This will help you as you work on redesigning your life as an introvert.

1. How to set goals

Imagine you could achieve anything you want and had no limitations whatsoever. What are the goals that, if achieved, would enable you to become the happiest you can be? Write down anything that comes to mind without judging it.

2. Select one goal

Select the one goal that, if achieved, would have the biggest impact on your life. Then circle it, because that will be your main goal.

3. Make it SMART

Too often, people set goals that are way too vague. When it comes to goals, the more specific, the better! So make sure you use the SMART goal method, which is explained below:

SMART stands for:

- Specific: What exactly do you want? What are you trying to achieve?
- Measurable: Can you assess the progress towards your goal? How will you know if you've achieved it?
- Achievable: Is it achievable? Is the timeframe realistic? Can you put in the effort required despite other responsibilities?
- Relevant: Is it in line with your values? Is it exciting to you?
- Time-bound: Do you have a clear deadline for your goal?

4. Break down your goals

If your goal is long-term, break it down into a yearly, monthly, weekly, and even daily goal. Now, ask yourself how confident you feel about your ability to achieve your goal. On a scale of 1 to 10, you want to be at a 7 or 8. If you're below this, try extending your timeline or making your goal smaller.

5. Implement one daily habit to support your goal

Implement one small habit that moves you towards your goal each day. For instance, my goal involves writing books, so I make sure I write every day no matter what.**Setting your goal**

1. How to set goals

What are the goals that, if achieved, would make you the happiest introvert ever?

-

-

-

-

-

2. Select one goal

Select the one goal that, if achieved, would have the biggest positive impact on your life and circle it. That will be your main goal.

Your one goal:

_____

_____

_____

3. Make it SMART

Too often, people set goals that are way too vague. When it comes to goals, the more specific, the better! So make sure you use the SMART goal methodology (specific, measurable, achievable, relevant, and time bound)

Your SMART goal:

_____

_____

_____

4. Chunk down your goals

If your goal is a long-term one, break it down into yearly, monthly, weekly, and even daily goals. See how you feel about each goal. On a confidence scale of 1 to 10, you want to be at a 7 or 8. If you aren't, extend the timeline or make your goal smaller.

Yearly SMART goal:

_____

_____

_____

Monthly SMART goal:

_____

_____

_____

Weekly SMART goal:

_____

_____

_____

5. Implement one daily habit to support your goal

What is one small daily habit that would help you achieve your goal?

My small daily habit:

_____

_____

_____

V. Transcending Your Introversion

I. Finding your passion

Answer the following questions to help you clarify your passion.

1) Who do you envy?

_____

_____

_____

2) What did you enjoy doing when you were a kid?

_____

_____

_____

3) What activities do you volunteer for at your current job? What about your previous jobs?

_____

_____

_____

4) What topic do you usually get excited about during conversations? When was the last time you got excited in a conversation?

_____

_____

_____

5) What is your unique way to contribute to the world? - Do you want to inspire? Entertain? Educate? Heal? Serve? Create art?

_____

_____

_____

6) According to you, what are your unique strengths? What is it that only *you* can do?

_____

_____

_____

2. Supercharging your passion

What skills must you develop to supercharge your passion?

-

-

-

-

What things beyond your comfort zone will you need to do to live a meaningful life?

-

-

-

-

-

-

-

3. Supercharging your ideas Are you capturing your ideas in an effective way? If not, what could you do to capture them more efficiently?

_____

_____

_____

Are you sharing your ideas and putting them out there? If not, what could you do to share your ideas and make a bigger contribution to the world?

_____

_____

_____

4. Introversion is not a label to wear

Could labeling yourself as an introvert (using your own definition of introversion) potentially harm your growth and fulfillment in life? If so, how?

_____

_____

_____

5. Becoming a leader

Now that you've read stories of introverted leaders, what would you say your biggest strength is? (thoughtfulness, perseverance, intensity etc.)

_____

_____

_____

What is one strength, that, if further developed, would make the biggest difference in your life?

_____

_____

_____

Notes